High Shelf

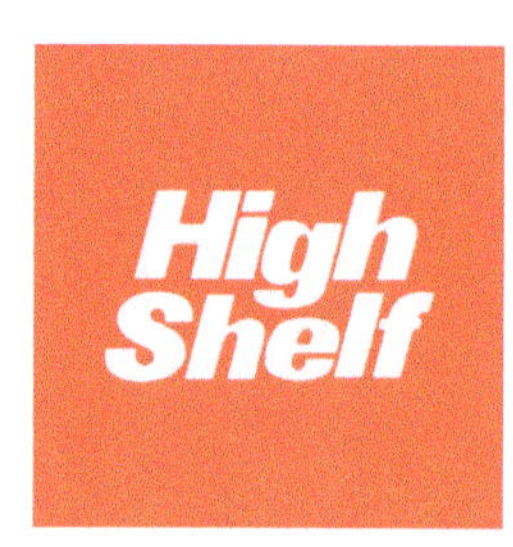

High Shelf Issue XV, February 2020
Portland, Oregon.
Copyright 2020, High Shelf Press

ISBN: 978-1-7342842-5-6

Cover Image by Maddie Fischer
Designed and Edited by C. M. Tollefson

High Shelf Press reserves all rights to the material contained herein for the contributors protection; upon publication, all rights revert to the artists.

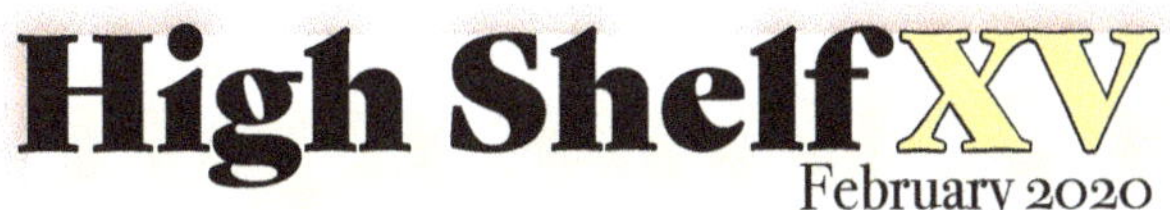

"We can speak simply,
affect a rhythmic pattern, engage
the lyric faculties, in advanced forms
masked as melodies..."

Rob Martinez

"... who would live
in this place

without some kind of
language..."
Amanda Leahy

Table Of Contents

her joke
Rashad Wright

i know a girl, with a standing ovation   where her voice used to be

she's tall enough to tear the light off the ceiling
she thinks the universe is round

sometimes i think she's right   when she knows she's wrong.

she laughs at her own jokes,   looks at me like i'm her best joke.
she'd make rust   think it was bronze.
she could turn water   into watercolor.
could turn right now into "are you done yet."

she makes me say   "i aint done yet."
makes me believe it . makes me scrape up my
"this is all i got" into a pile of "we got this"

she is a girl   with a hook for a heartbeat.

she is the best kind   of worst person.

she's been forever and back . she saw tomorrow , yesterday . she likes really bad episodes of
really good shows . her smile can't keep a secret . she thinks she's a secret . she's not . she's just
a note in a song that holds itself too hard.

she cracks, is torn   has thorns and has named each one
has enough holes   to call herself a dreamcatcher.
she is whole and catches dreams

but me i'm just a guy
writing poems
about a girl
with a shine
where she thinks
her broken is.

The Anatomy of My Debris

Henry Stanton

This delirious poem is a piece of trash
it has arms and legs a head
a drooling head
its feet clomp from the weight of being
detritus
the body contorts from
the pain of being discarded.

The eyes pressed into this fool face are plastic caps.
The hair on its clumsy head is composite small bits of plastic line
weed whacking line fish line
plastic tabs and pulls and cable ties.

My debris is a work of art.

My debris is an artist with cigarette butt fingers
and gumchew toes.
Sunscreen sluffing skin
Tear off float off sheets of greasy coral-killing skin.
A rain of the artist pilfering resources clogs
Seas and bays and rivers and my home stream
chokes off the ocean of all creation
Shedding bits of garbage from the cloak of its being like Appleseed.

Dear gods can't we burn this body as an offering?
The rank and the poisonous and the forlorn given up to you?
Let our crooked smokes climb to your nostrils through the black ruined air.
Let us be rid of everything.

Still present with me it enters in unexpectedly

Kristin Withers

it was the first cool day when I was suicidal to meet you
oh, songworm descant & charmed
there I was sitting in the mirror — hideous & silent mirror

tell me in broken metaphor & it grows in broken duplicate

the effervescent dancer forgets to lament the dream,
tangible before him — babbling babbling brooks
sing to me in shallow lacerations with no additional text

& if I wished it in depth & if I wished it were saline
then they would be anything instead
numb openings — oh, what about me possibly cannot

tell me in broken metaphor & it grows in broken duplicate

laborious love — too far in long, I have lost my way
so I had lain down for it to touch me
fall — your reaching finger, the very last leaf

Memoir Of Ghosts

Cree Cullars

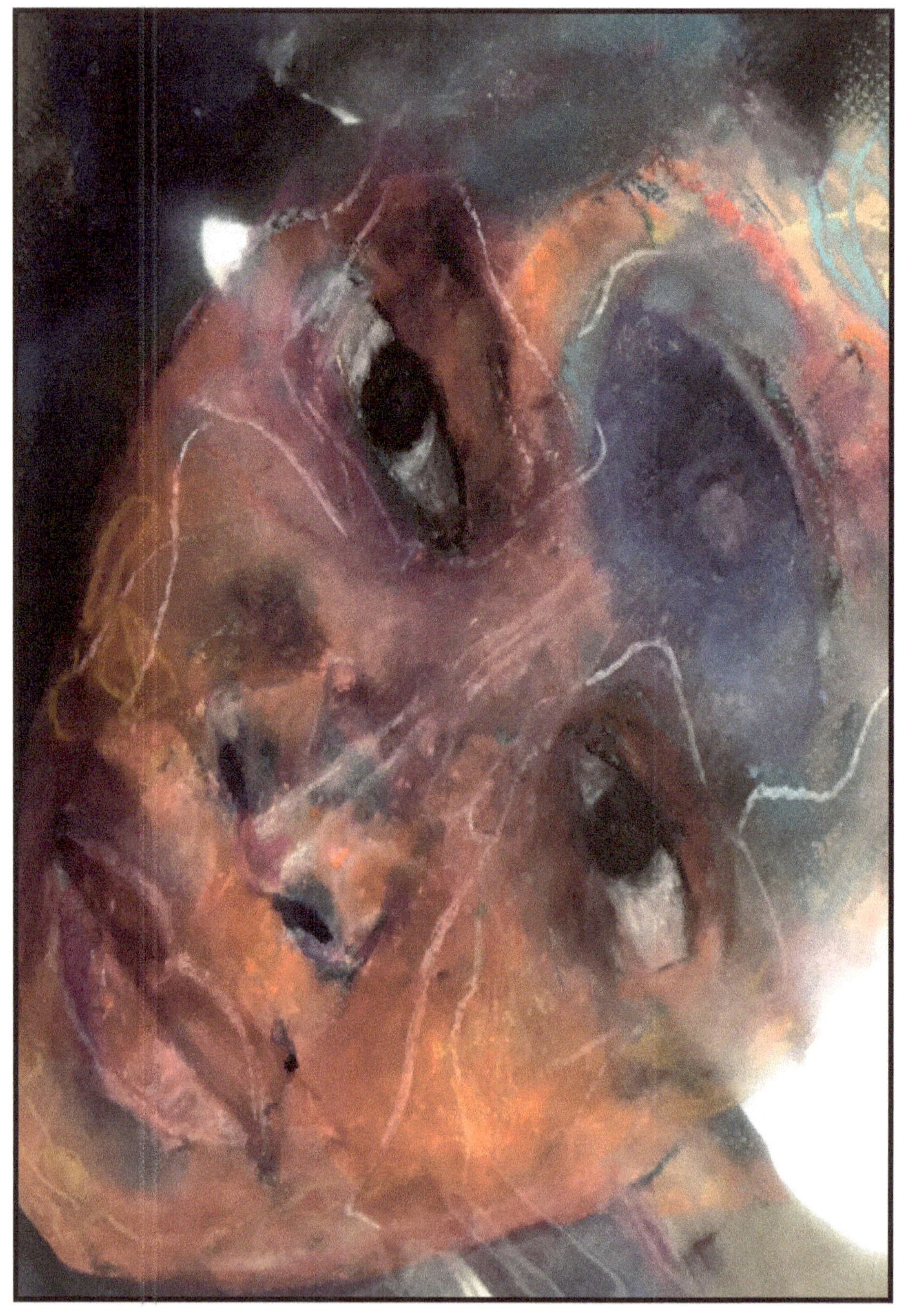

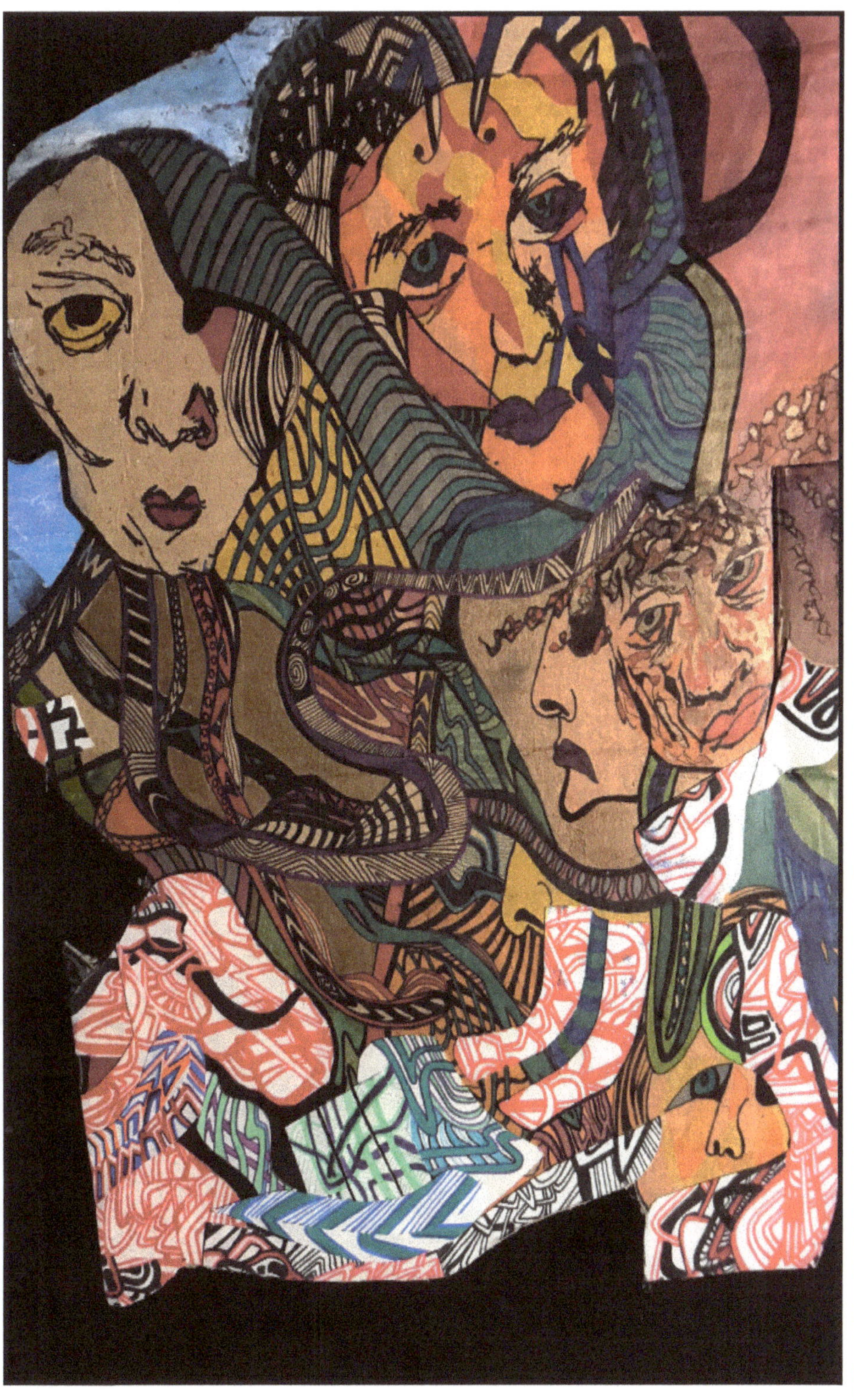

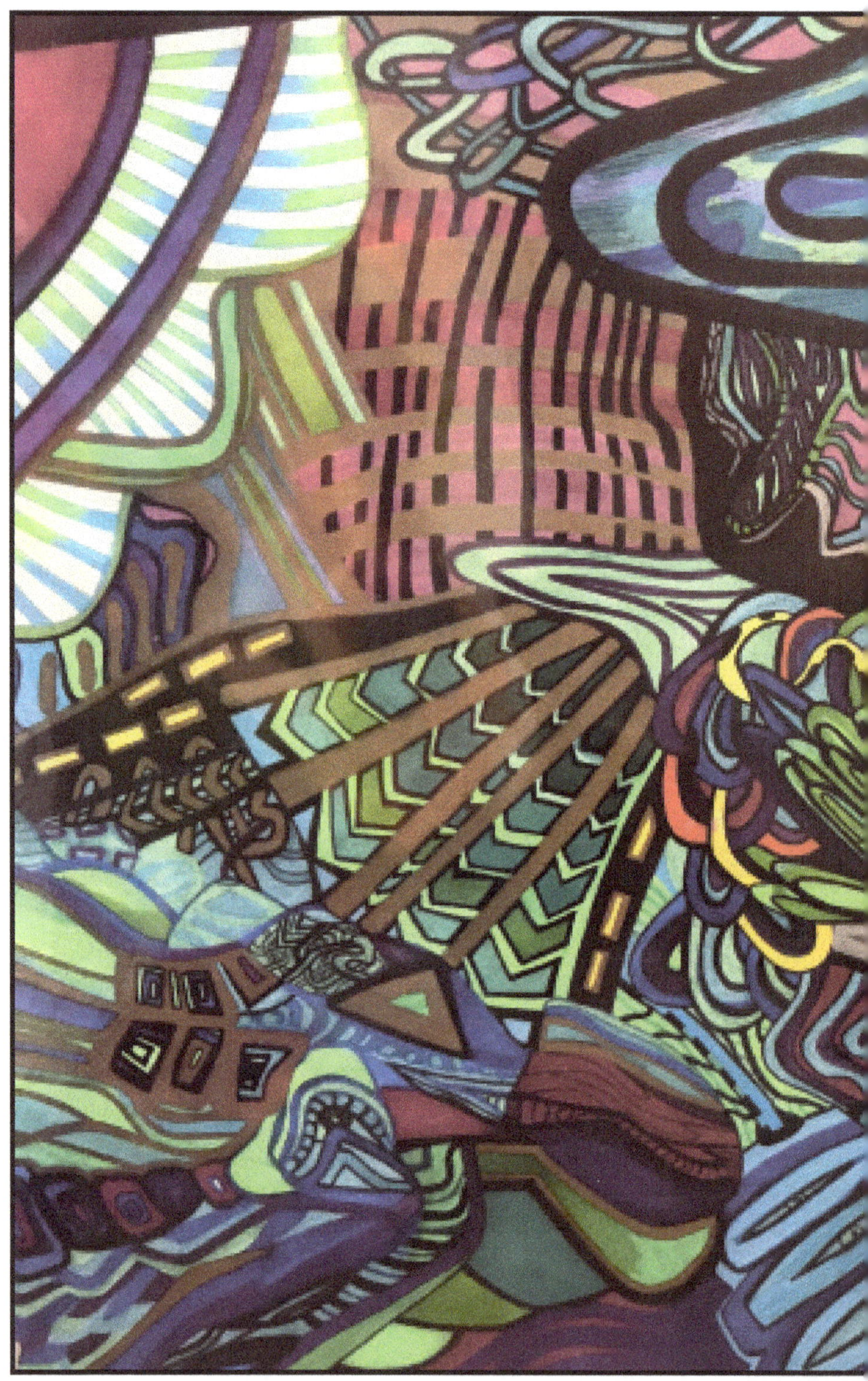

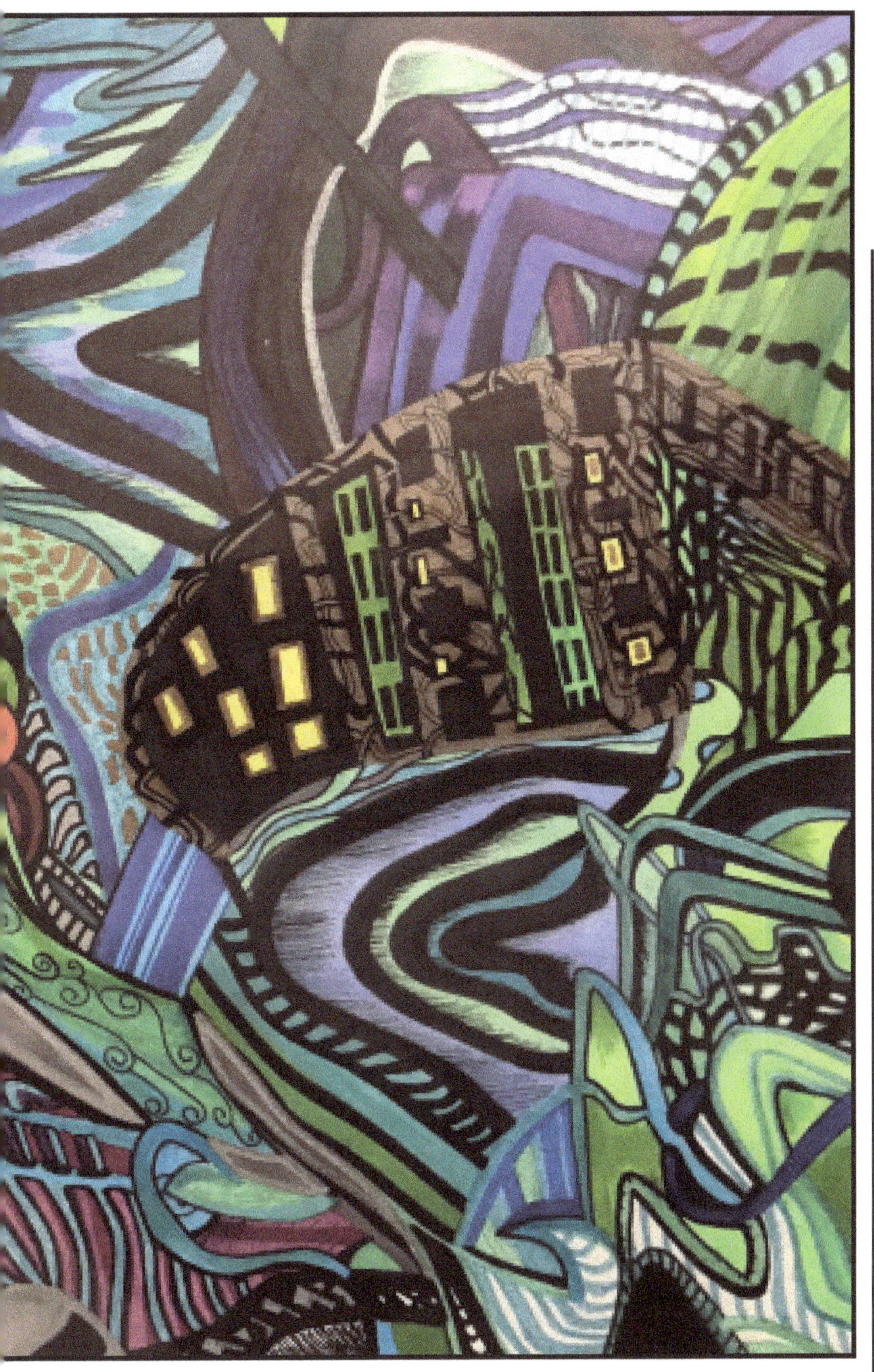

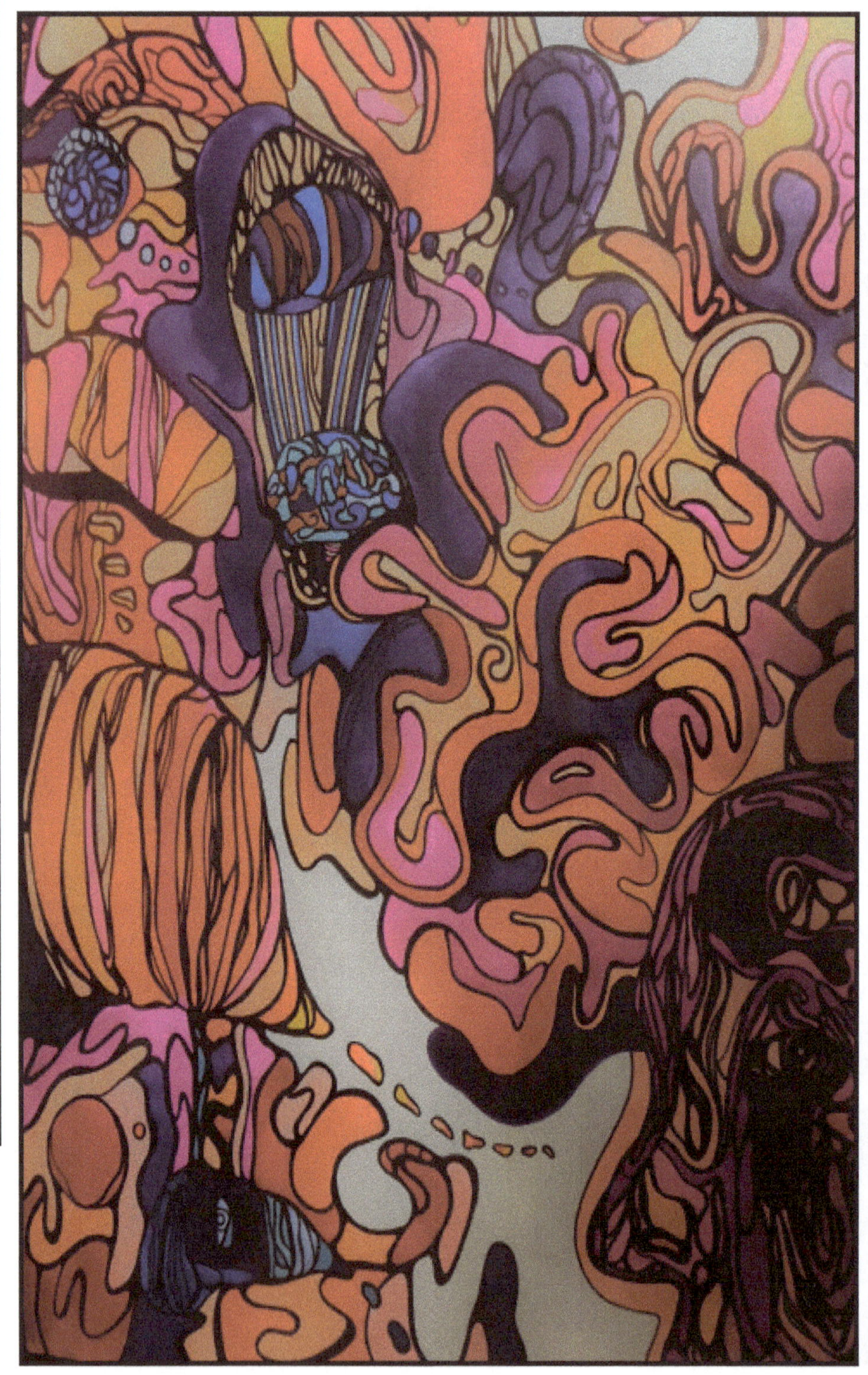

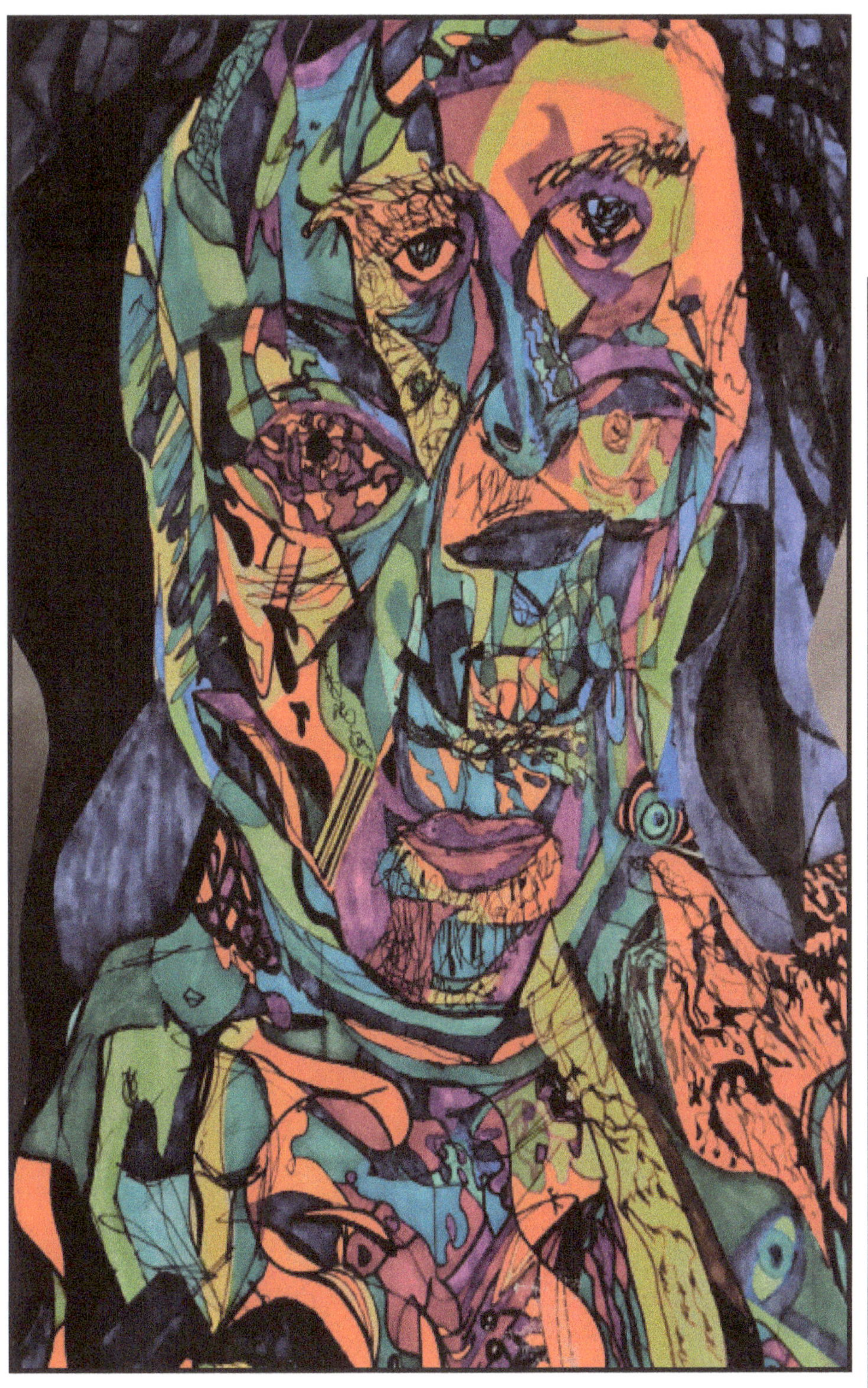

Windows

Emily Capers

Thank the Norsemen for their crashing longships landing on the western sands of Europe in 843. Their raid led them to a place of worship where prayer and saints repeated themselves in the window of the church

        Jesus   a mother and child   a cross
        in amber   in sapphire.

The Vikings named it *vindauga.*
   Vindr meaning "wind."
   Auga meaning "eye."

And perhaps they would have chosen a different name if the images did not obscure the invitation from the white man inside, holding faith in his hands because words have power.

Centuries passed when the artist understood *vindauga* to mean that the eyes are the window to the soul.

Inside the coffee shop, the artist sits at a table alongside the window. "I need inspiration." Smudges map the entire glass, held together by a metal picture frame. The windows ledge, a single plank of wood, holds the artist's supplies: a pen, a notepad, and
   for colored girls who have considered suicide/when the rainbow is enuf.

When my grandfather died, I wrote him a letter. I sat at the desk behind the only window in my bedroom, with a second-story view of pansies and bloodroot because there's beauty in words. Because words have power. The Bible tells me
   ask, and it shall be given.

When I was younger, my parents would convince me to sit on the front porch and watch the storm with them. The slits of the plastic chair pinched my bare thighs as I stood when a crack of lightning told me to go back inside. In the living room, behind the glass and the panes, the wonders of nature performed for me. In her selfish way, she shook trees, buildings, and allowed her light to strike and enter the family room once every few minutes.

It was Édouard Bénédictus in 1909 who dropped and shattered a jar of oil in his bedroom. After finishing the painting, he created safety glass, that when struck, simply bulges and bends.

During family trips, I'd glare forward, from the backseat and through the windshield. Even on a sunny day, I'd keep watch for threatening clouds or
   ADULT TOYS
"Oh, that's real nice." Everyone laughed.
   those who look through windows grow dim (Ecclesiastes 12:3)

It wasn't until after the funeral that I realized the Lord was right.

The Ancient Romans built their windows by flattening glass jars into small, thick sheets which now hang inside of my apartment, like paintings. I watch them as vehicles pass below on the slick pavement. Car horns. Any horn. Instruments trying to get in tune, C or C#. The voice of the crosswalk tells me

   Go. Go. Go. Walk. Go. Go.

At the market with you after staring at Delaroche's La Jeune Martyre (1855) when I thought I was looking for Waterhouse's Ophelia (1894) but was really looking for Millais's Ophelia (1851-2) on the Internet

Erin Bennett

Green wind in May. The first leafy things to poke out of the dirt, plucked. And gathered in weepy
bundles on the local produce shelf. Already ochre at the edges.
The mist machine hisses. The next shelf over, the baskets are plump with tacky green apples and
bitter tangerines. Impossible pineapples. This local stuff, meanwhile, glistening products of melted
snow and occasional sun beginning to wilt and bruise, untethered. Thirsty.
Candy beets, green kale, purple cabbage, velvet endives and little radishes.
Pause here. French breakfast radishes, *Raphanus raphanistrum* (wild) or *raphanus sativus* (cultivated).
There. Perfect smallness. Their color, blush.
The color of early mornings as we spin closer in proximity to the sun. Shaped like robins eggs.
The cows across the river mooed all night, do you remember? We were trying to sleep as they cast
their brimming voices against the hillside. Hm. Those cows. We must have slept some, anyhow.
Sleep. Breath over your lips, river rushing over the dam, that endless mooing, mooing, mooing,
the neighbor's dog whining from the third floor window. I even thought the stars were shuffling,
shaking their legs, unsettled. I try to be silent. I think of silence.
I can't help it. I've heard there is nothing more poetic than the death of young woman, or so.
I can't help it. I bathe in it, like orchid water. The image. The image of my body, growing cool now in
the evening, like it does. You, laying my cool body right down in the earth on a bed of radish greens.
Nothing else though, an Ophelia's burial, dress pressed in the mud, held by mama earth,
at night, in secret, only a few witnesses, my laced fingers and blue wrists all tangled
and tied in the flowers that drowned us/me/her.
Anyway, on a bed of radish greens, sprinkled all around with their pebbly seeds,
like the grains of gray sand on the beach of a frozen lake, yes, that's how they are. Then a bit of sod
to cover me. Would you, would you curse the stars? Don't tell me. But either way, water me
and the radish seeds when you think of it. Water us until the sky is in puddles at your feet. Then wait.
There will be sprouts on this side of the mud, Ophelia's and mine. They will grow a bright peppery
taproot, pink and alive. And the next spring, there will be a small harvest.
Up with the radish greens will rise one free and organic woman, brushing the mud off, untangling,
stretching, walking, on a pink moon night, like this, barefoot and dew-covered among the radish flow-
ers, white petals with purple center, *Raphanus raphanistrum.*
Following the cow's call—ahh, hmm, that's why they moo so. Those cows.
I will come through the woods, across the river, past the neighbor's house—you'll hear the dog bark
when I rustle the lilacs—and back to you. Just as every morning. Just as this morning.
And now I find you the next aisle over, counting all the kinds of cooking oils.
Olive, extra virgin, coconut, avocado, hazelnut, grape seed.
I think you are going to laugh. Pause here.
There is nothing more poetic than the death of a young woman, maybe so,
except, I think, for her life, and all she hungers.

Working Days
Zoltan Kegyes

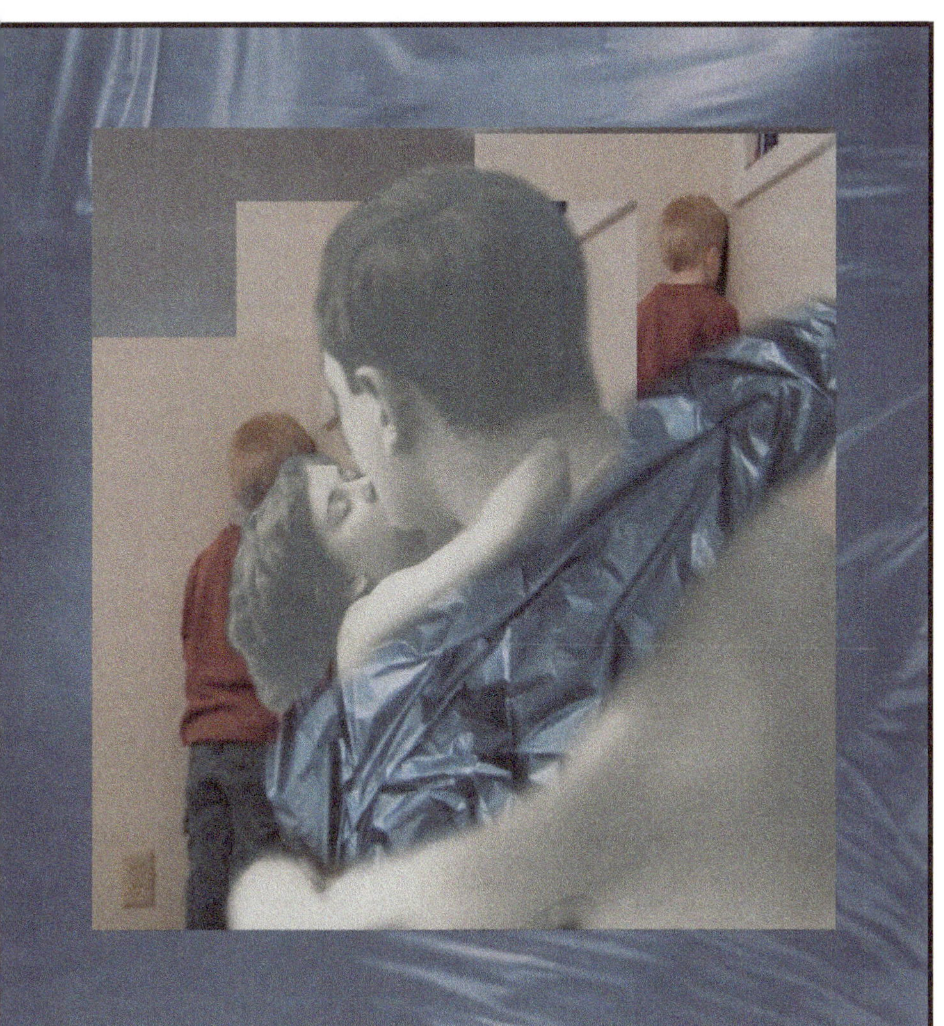

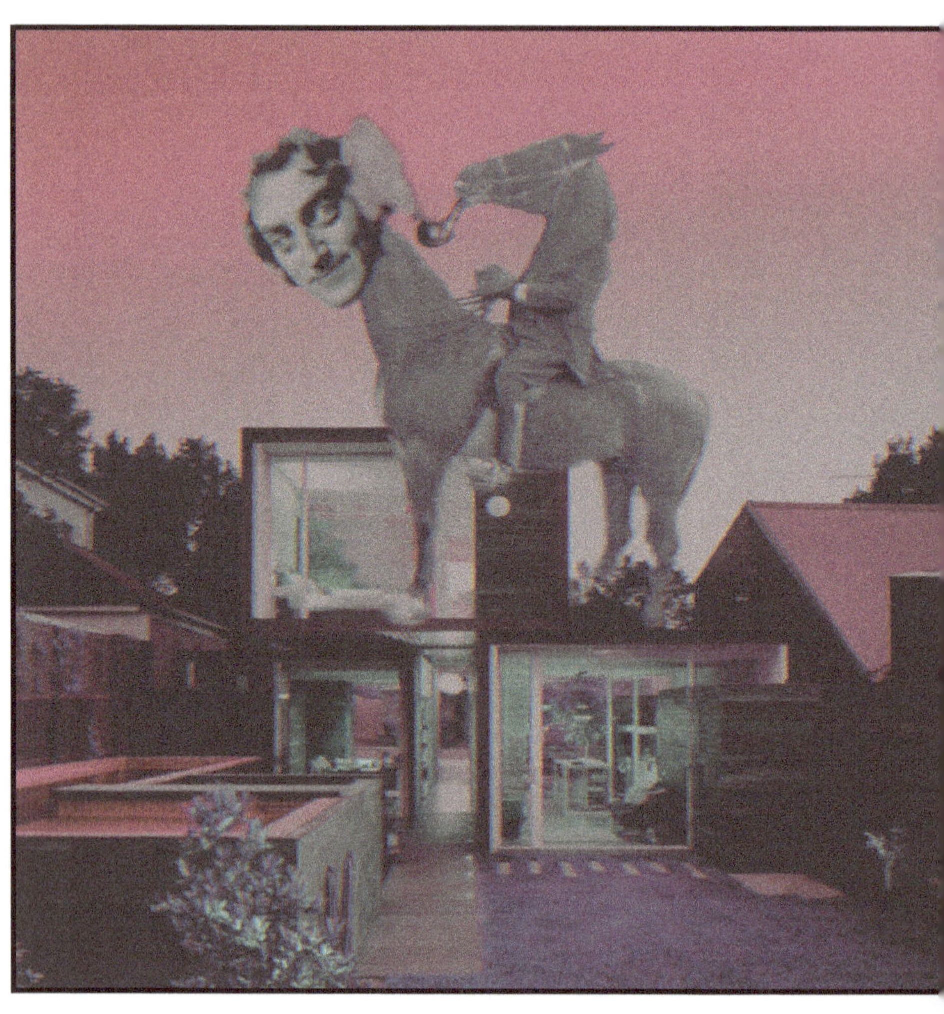

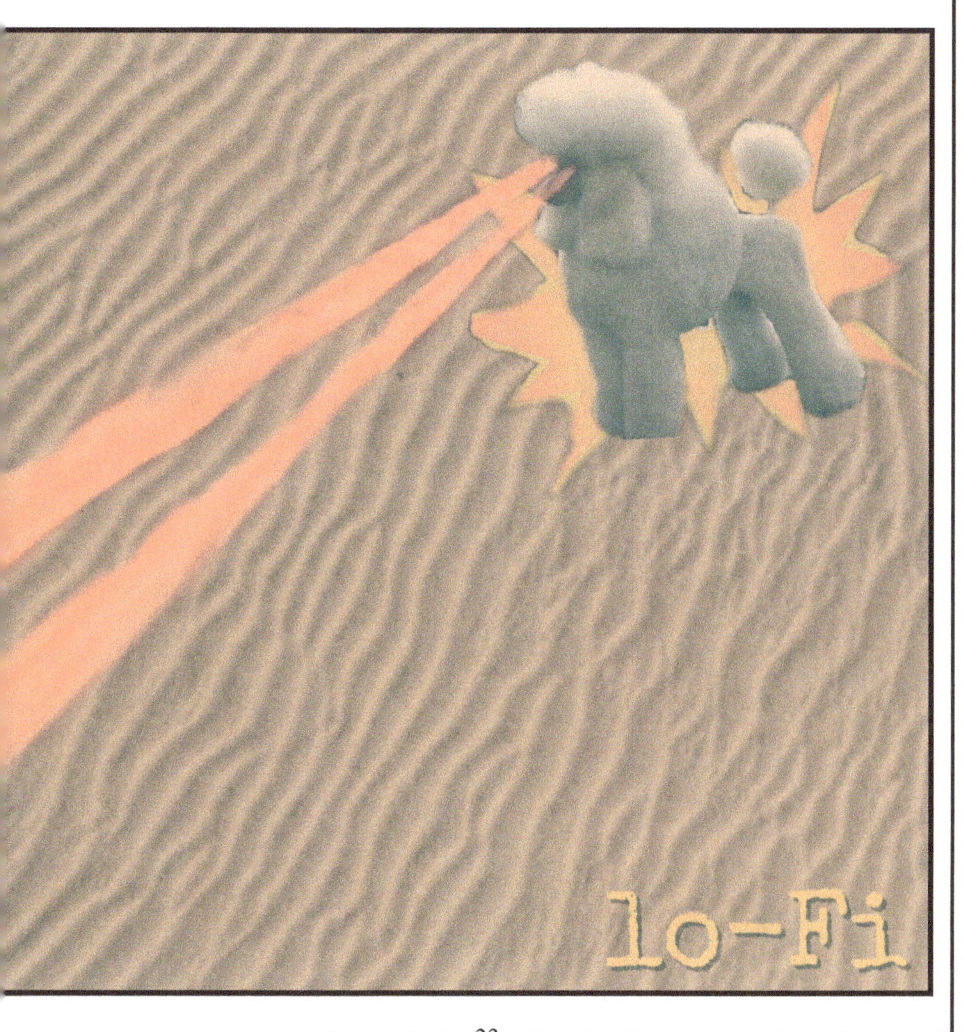
lo-Fi

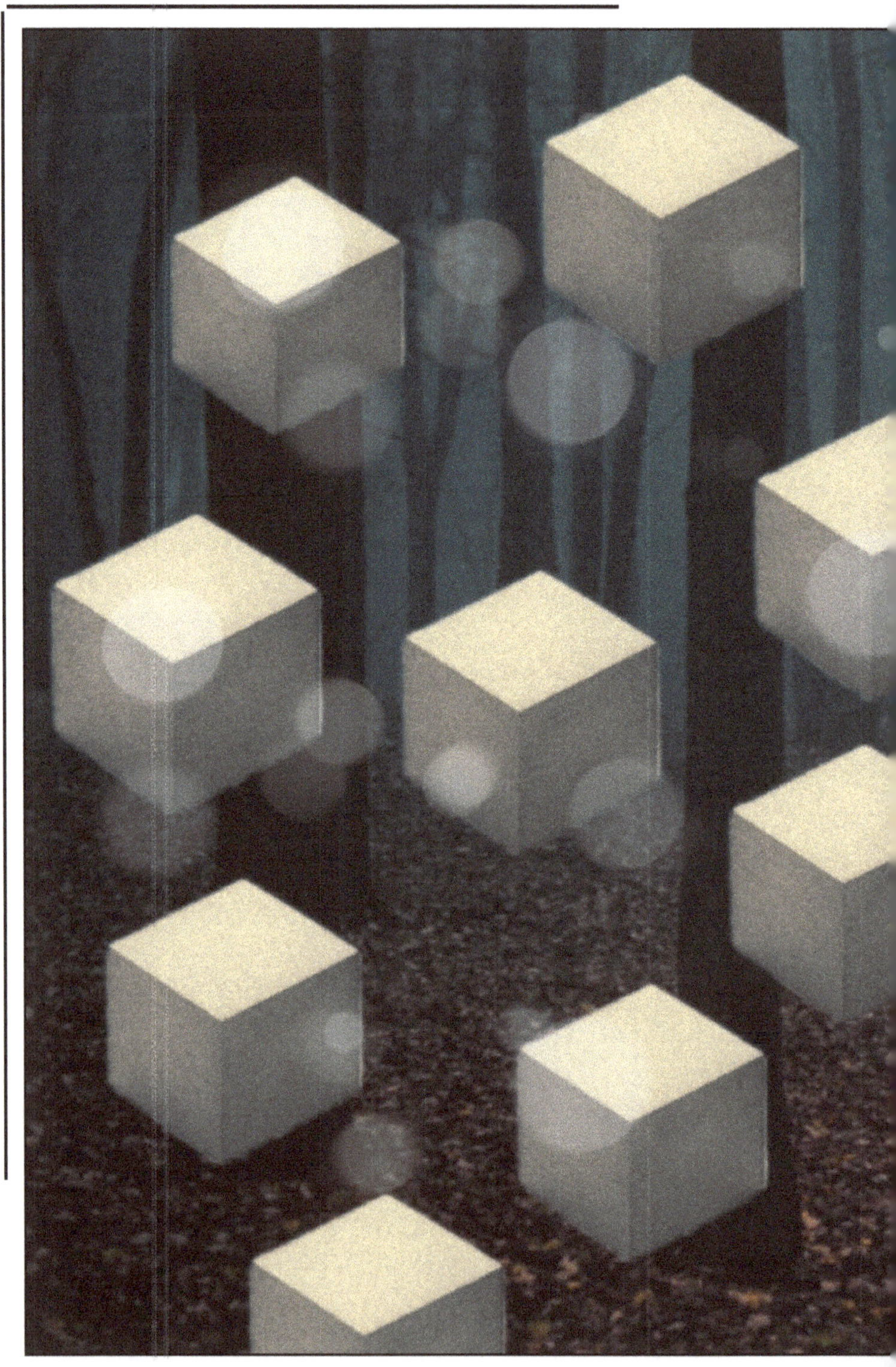

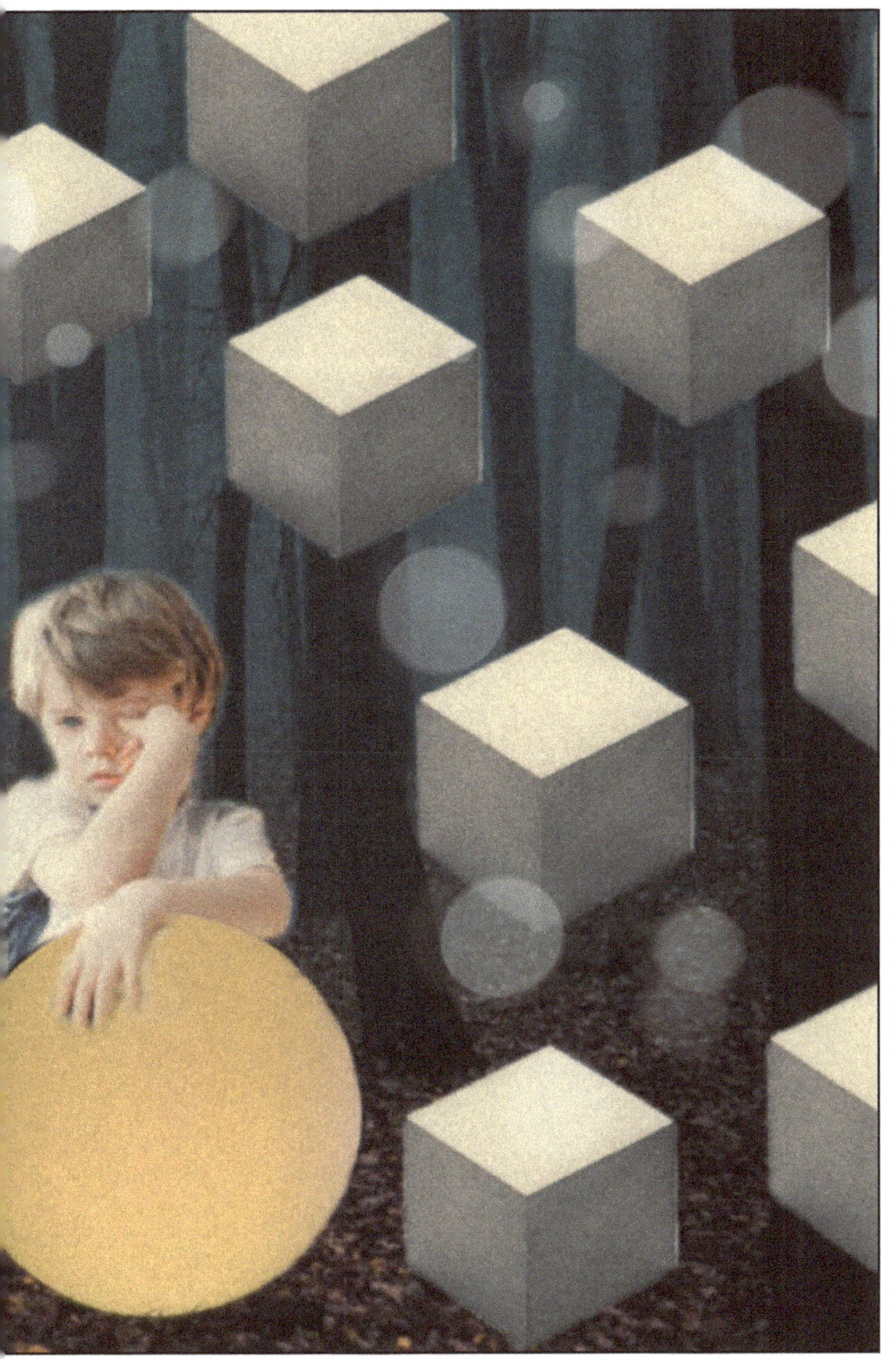

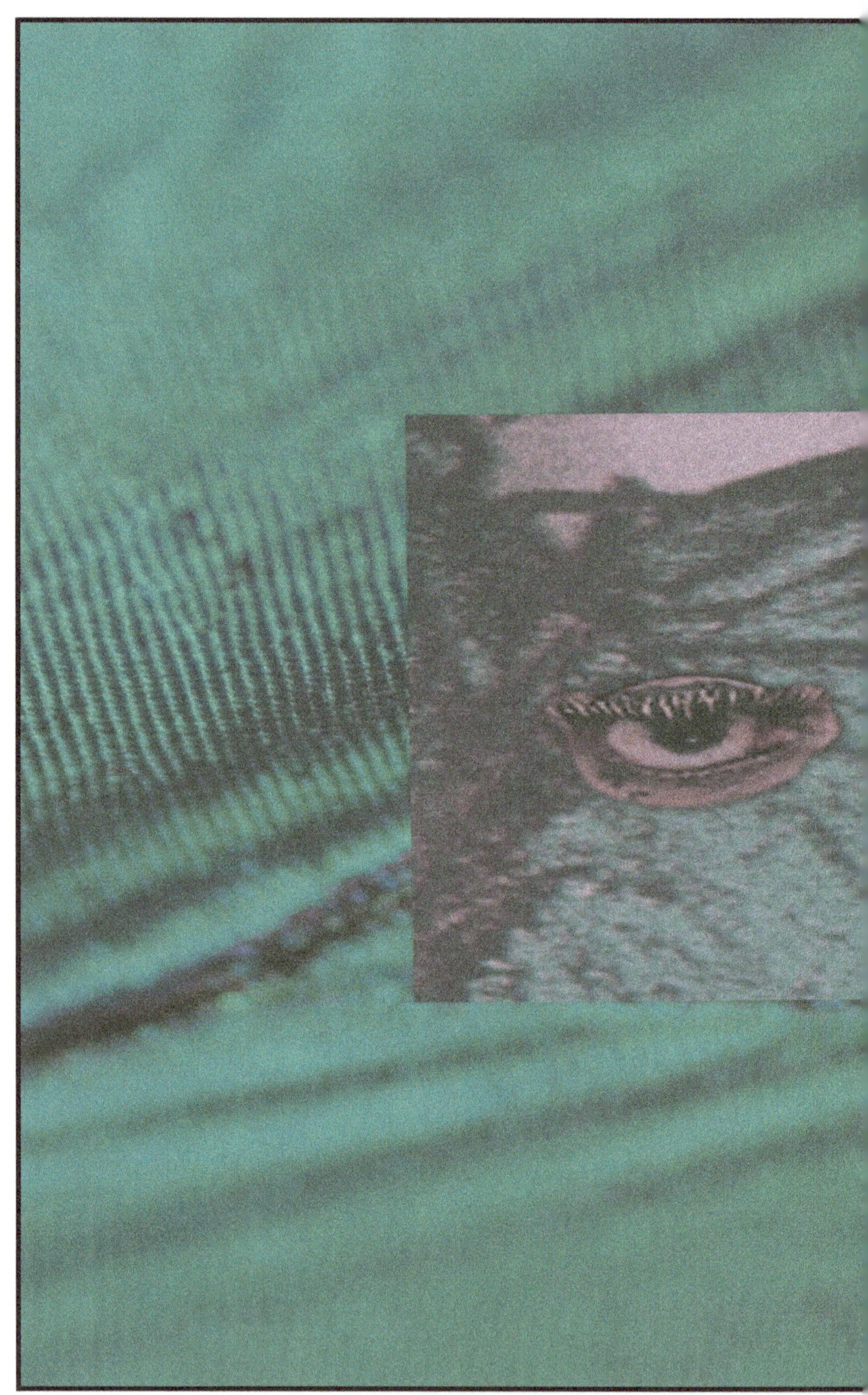

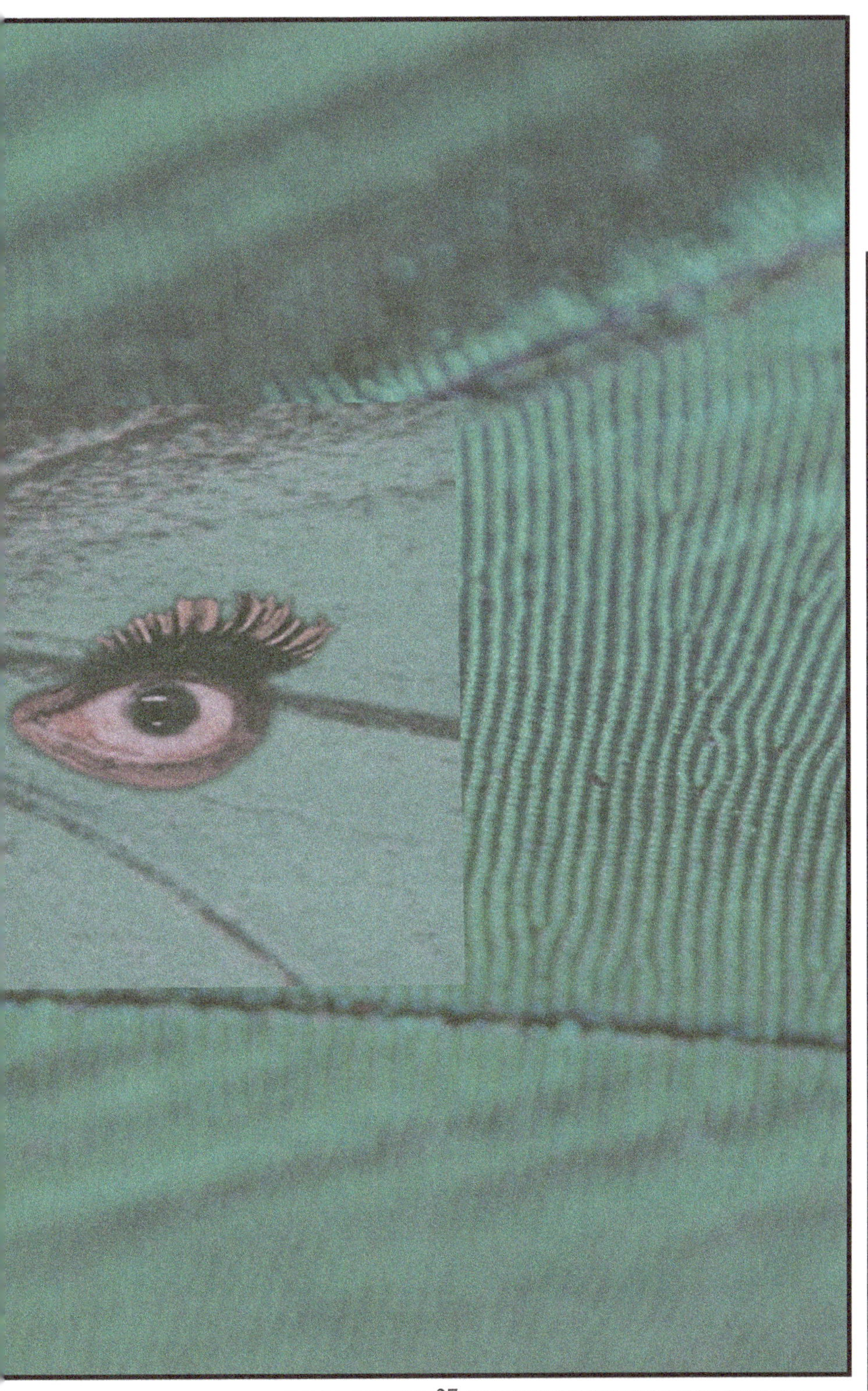

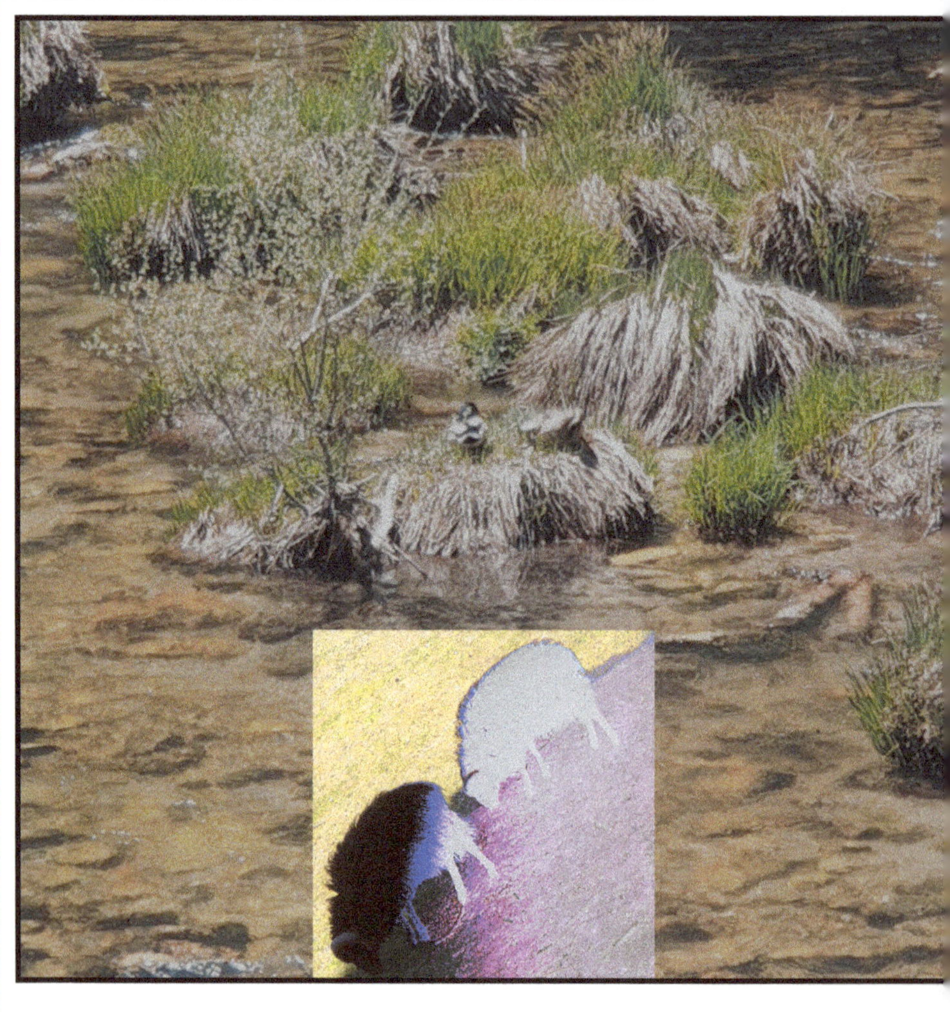

MEGARA, DREAM CHILD

Stephen Herman

1.   The Vision

Getting under the wire fence
lifting the latch on the barnyard door
scurrying into boxes   corners
                              fitting in

There was this need to rummage through
attics   cellars   eaves
places immediate to new things

There was this fleeting urge
to stroke the sun
to get the hands the arms the whole back
                        pressing down

and then there was this slipping out
like moths slowly from the hard-shelled pupa

2.   The Journey

At first when the fever broke
and the mad dream drifted like clouds
across the plains I came to you

silent   void   the melancholic fetus
wrapped in swaddling clothes its only shroud

and I thought of turning myself over
like a leaf or the soil and following the child down
the limbs to the trunk   the roots

to the mouth of the tree and leaving her there
where the earth begins and the glow worms pass
like sentinels in the night

3.   The Return

An egg in the eye of death
the sweet and gentle carcass of a calf
inundated with fleas

I speak of a child whose unlit eyes
are the wells of the world
whose ears are caves   whose lips and skin
suffer the ruins of dried up springs

I speak of my own facelessness
the negative print of it wrinkled and stained

And I bring myself back to you
Over the field   picking my way

Like a songless bird in the calm of the storm

Etymology
Heather Quinn

1. Aminion: Greek and Latin root of English *amniotic*

    a. bowl to catch the blood of a sacrificial body
(ex., lamb)

    b. sheath to protect a fetus of vertebrates in embryonic development
(ex., serpent, dove, human)

2. Amniotic

    a. thin membrane forming a closed liquid sac
for embryos and fetuses of mammals, reptiles and birds
(ex., lion, lizard, loon)

3. Amnesia

    a. the word in ancient Greek was *amnestia*
as in a wrong being forgiven
(see *amnesty*)

    b. forgetfulness, *a = not*
& mnesia = remembering

    c. loss of memory usu. due to brain injury, shock, repression, fatigue or illness

    d. gap in one's memory

    e. selective overlooking or ignoring of events that are not favorable to one's
purpose or position
(ex. high crimes)

4. Amniotic ≠ Amnesia

    etymologically speaking
there is no connection

    amniotic is likely the older of the two words

    a. first there was life

(ex., gestation placenta blood bone breath hunger mother umbilical cut suck)

b. then came forgetting

5. **Amnesty**

when we claim amnesia
what will we say killed the serpents, doves, lions, lizards, loons
what will we say killed the children
will we use the aminion of our hands to cup sacrificial blood
what of the question of high crimes; the question of amnesty
(see *extinction*)

New Illustrations
Maddie Fischer

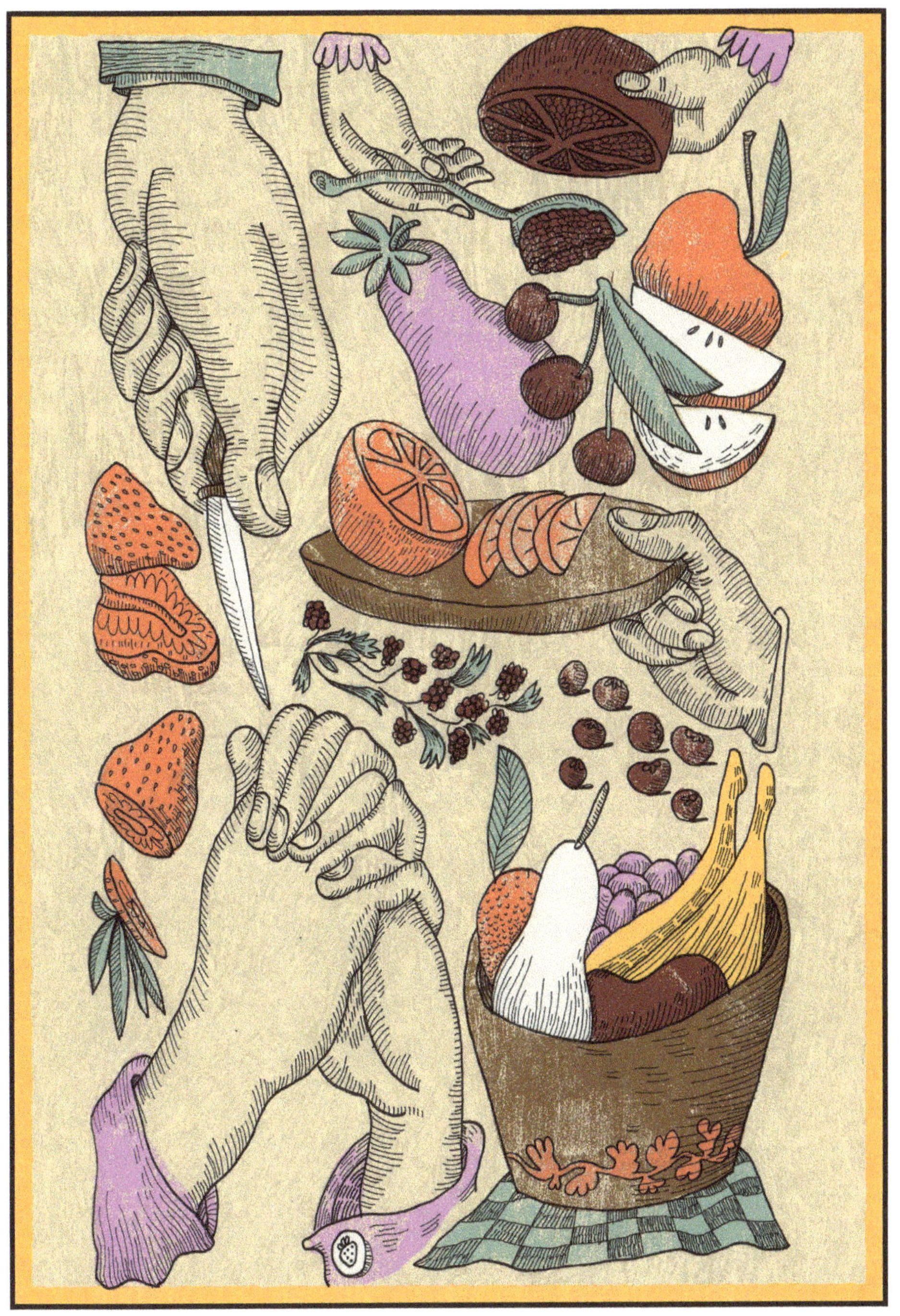

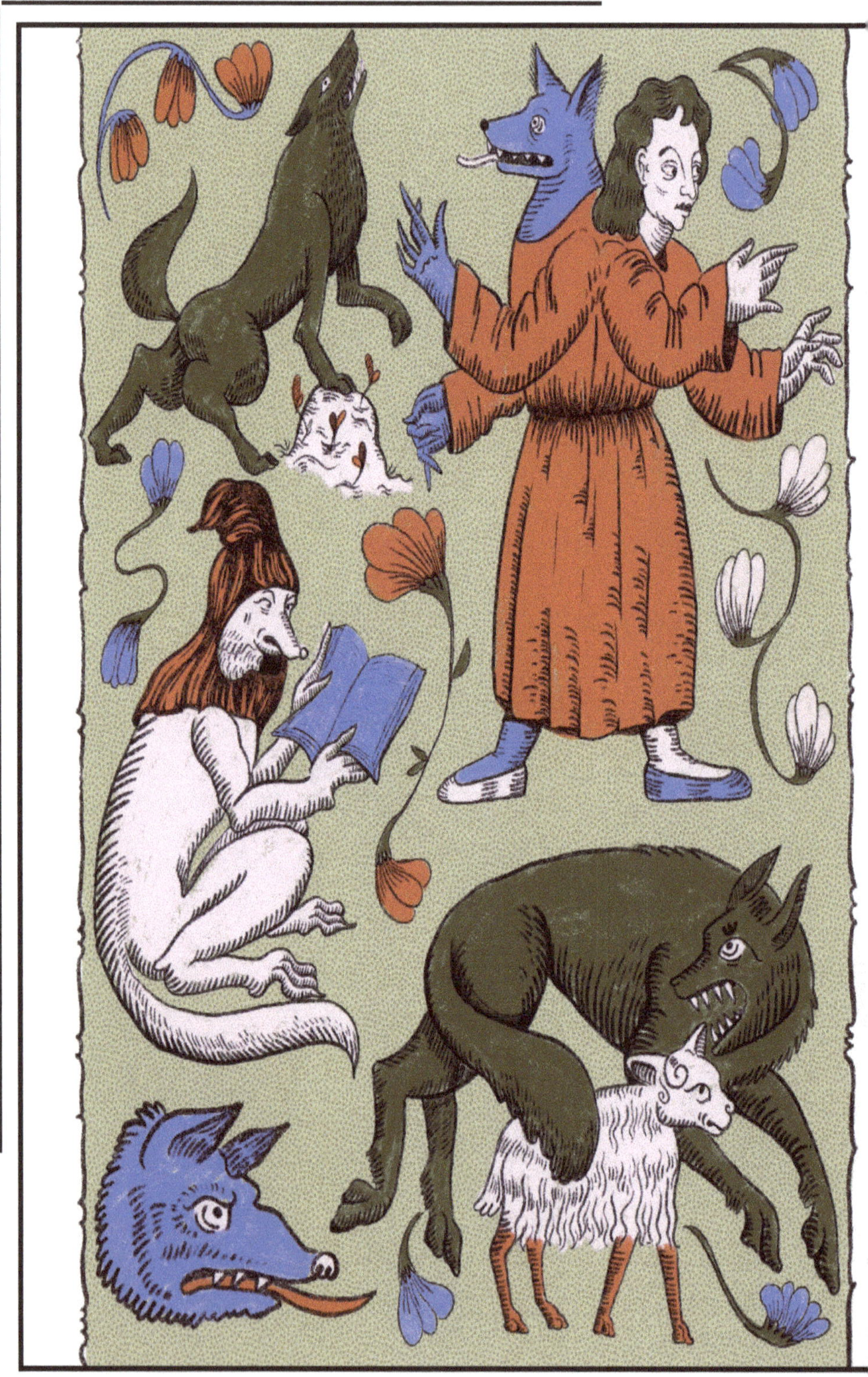

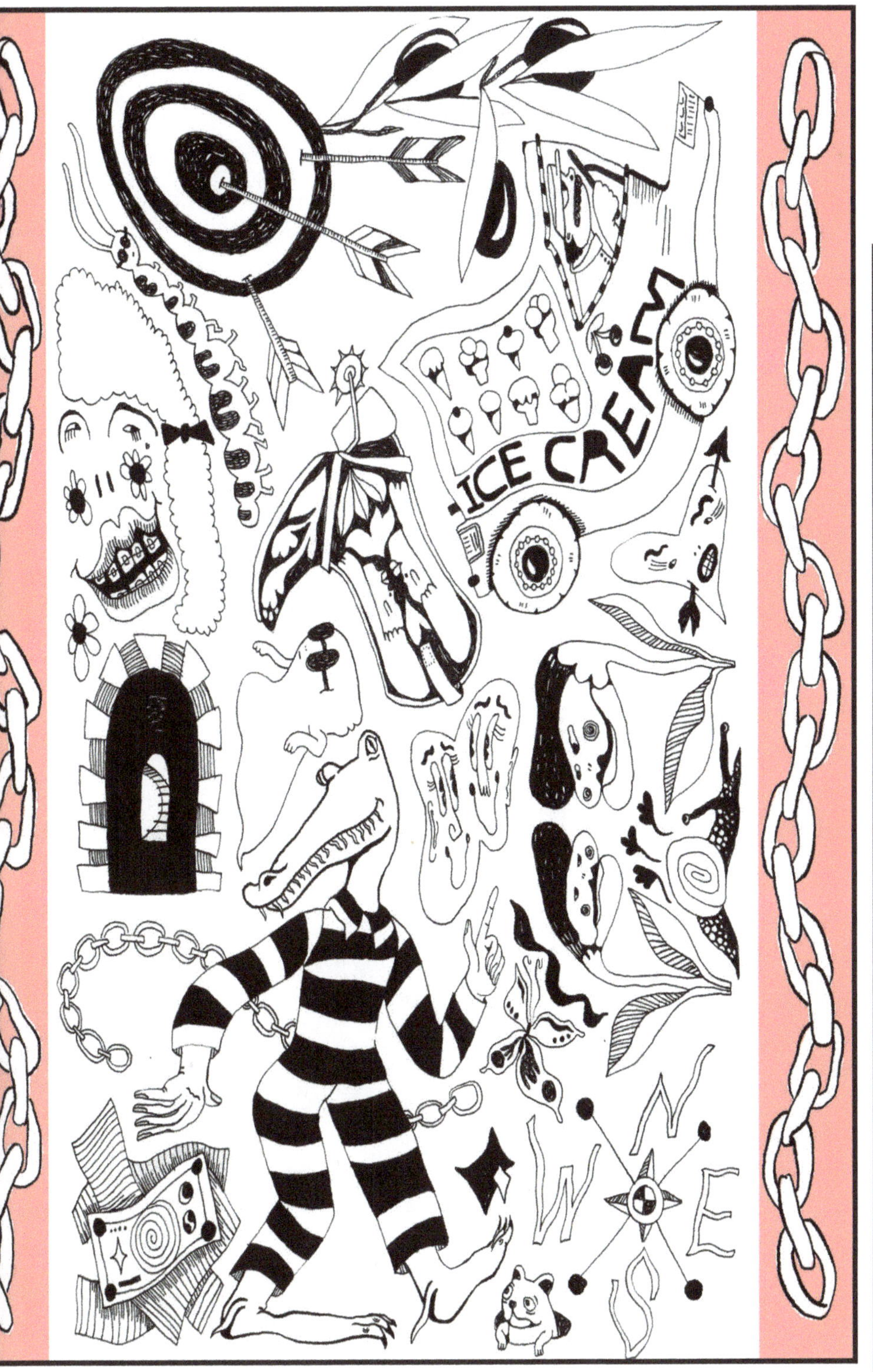
ICE CREAM
N
W
S
E

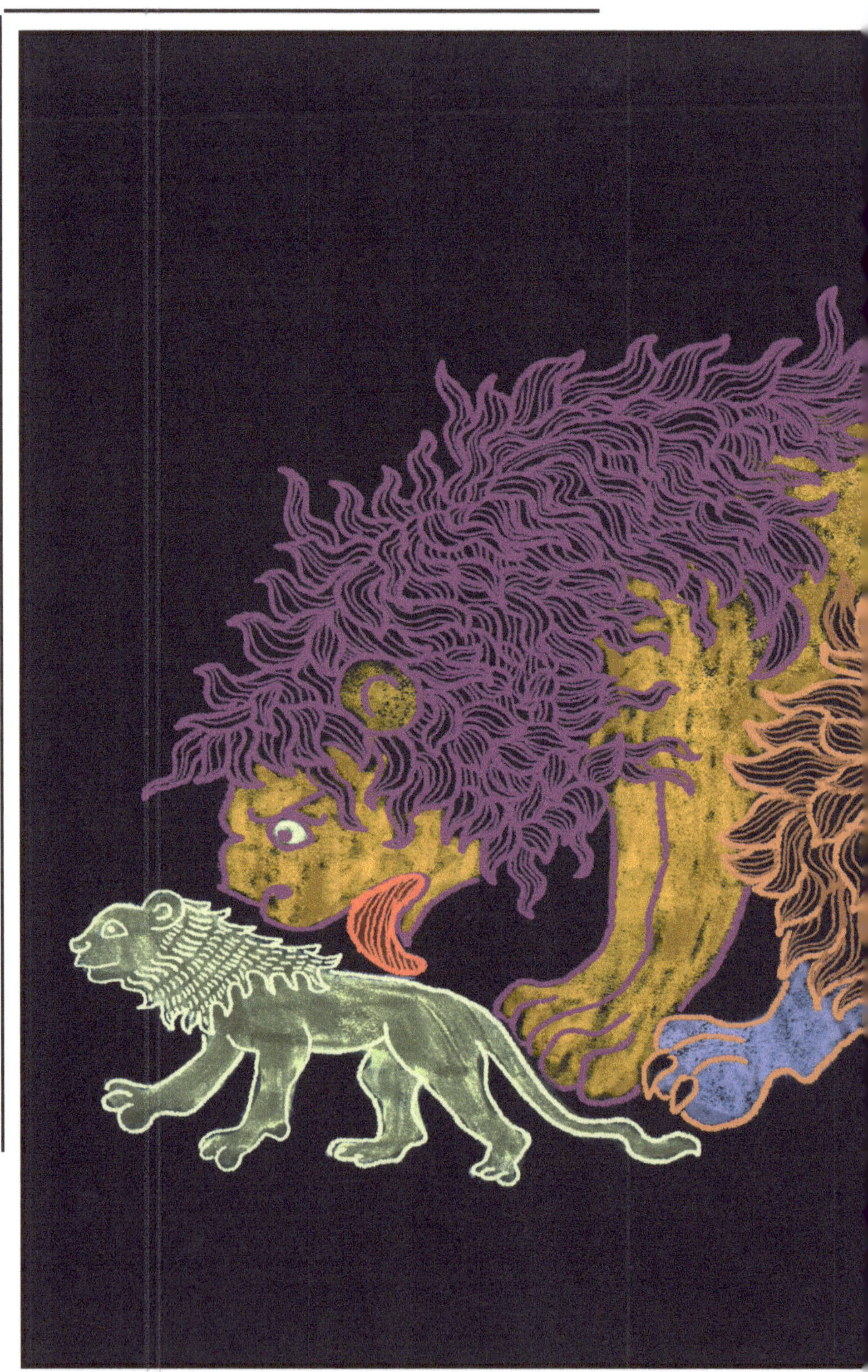

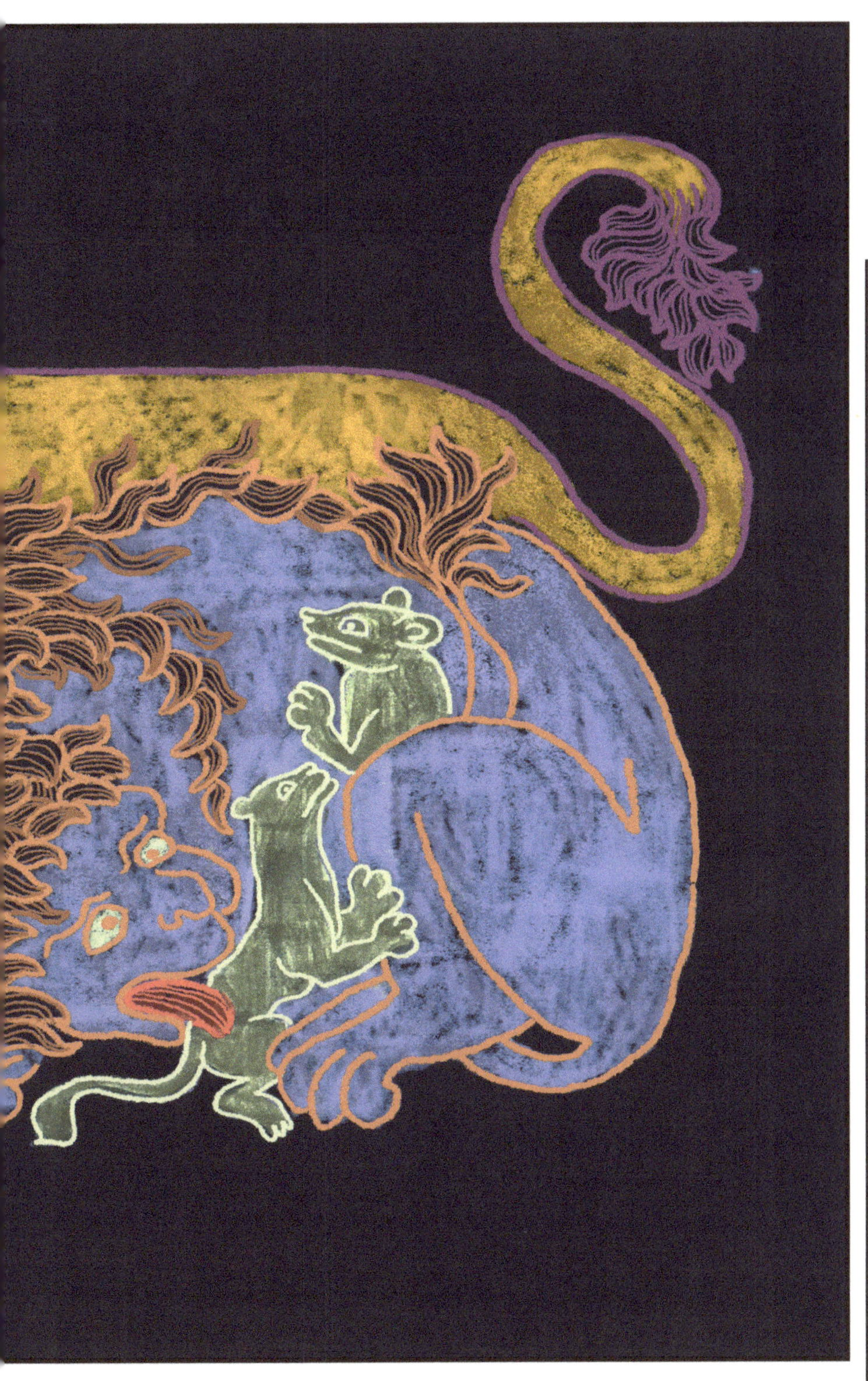

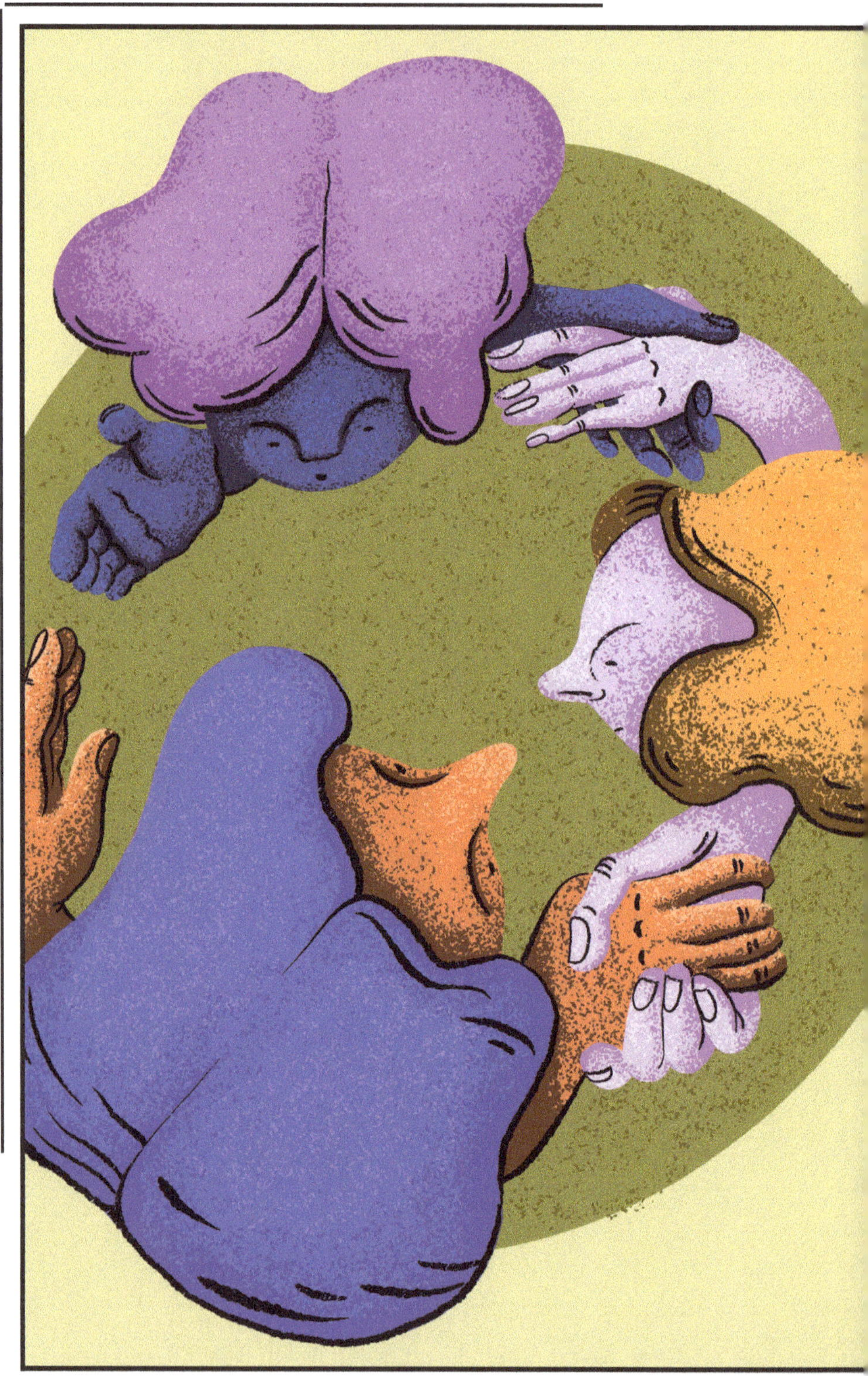

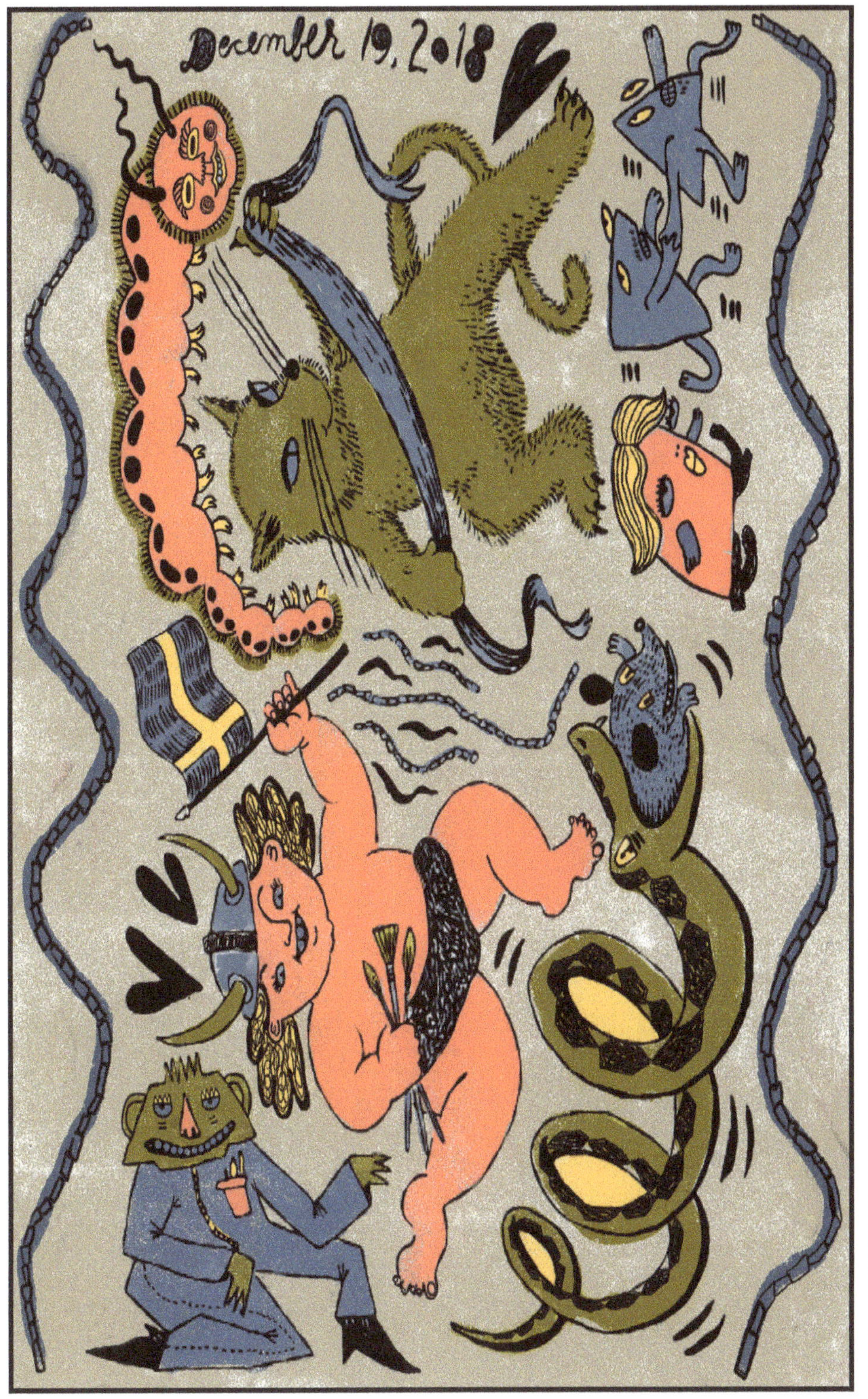
December 19, 2018

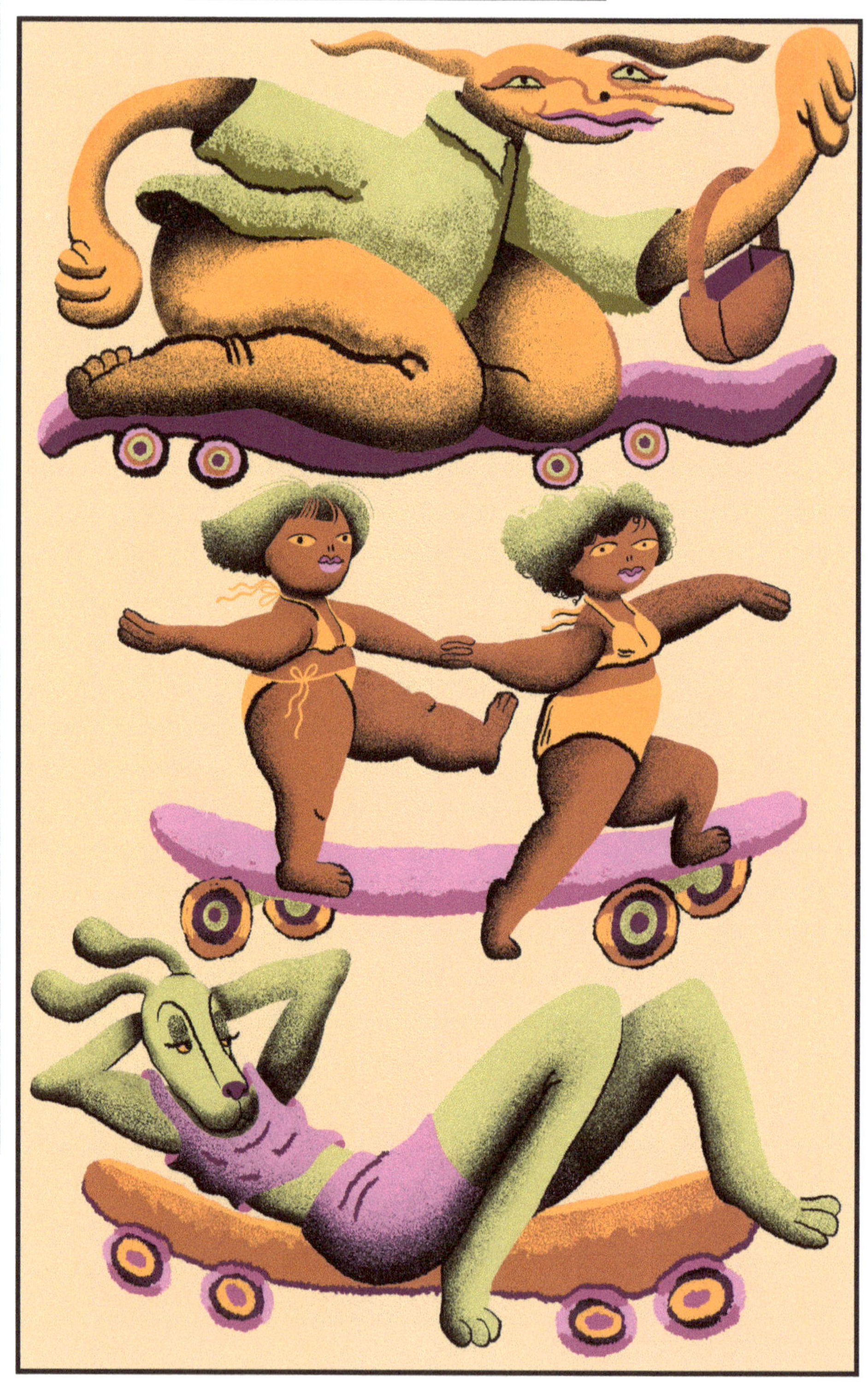

Of Course

Rob Martinez

We can speak simply,
affect a rhythmic pattern, engage
the lyric faculties, in advanced forms
masked as melodies
dance between the awful things
prioritize our problems
like spices
and allow a two week window of grief

in retrospect
we were too young to process it
innocent of spiritual wrongdoing
cleansed now, too, with homogenous aging
eased into opinions like loafers
to dream a dream of relative anxiety
to fear my unimportant death

We can hardly swell!
past the engorged borders of our souls
we can hardly be more kind!
or circuitous philanthropic
take a bastard coffee
spilt through sheets of tribal testimony
short shrift to the infidels! pity in a paper cup
the TV beamed it

Of course hypocrisy
Of course, chanting
       Sadnesses
               unique   colors
different
static   mosaics
special sauces
glazed over eyes
       like
              an artisan

Of course heredity
Of course, to adventure
blind open for the unjealous

to zipline past the sick hut
feed me mommy
feed me

merigolds
small children
respiratory filth
beautiful children
one penny, two pennies
feed me

the hackneyed songs
I long to sing.

The System is Ruined

Eros Livieratos

A silver spoon; a crack
pipe. I love you, pieces
and all. God is a green
thumbed woman—pierced
nose like a bull, eyes like
stuffed gray boulders.
Chrysanthemum hands—
petals that shape earth to heart.

Lance of Longinus,
phallic and misplaced.
Tonsils like an arched high
way—I want to swallow.

My throat is a guarded clitoris;
the sidewalk on 14th
is a battleground. If
a purple hued comet
broke our monotony like fist
through arcade screen or
small hands to cosmic dust
back into quarks or the
magic between the fingertips
of a pianist; I would still
love you. Suffering and
all.

Tibia: support beam,
trash can foundation;
dreams of pataphysics, dreams
abject—sullen from trials of justice.
I repent to the wind; to the
marrow and the soil, the blood
yet to flow from a river, bleeding
Bacchus red—drowning in polka-dot pollution green

We'll be in touch

Ellis Scott

"Thank you for coming in."

"Thank you for having me."

"Bauhaus 93 is an original font choice for a resume."

"Thank you I'm glad you like it."

"And thank you for the attached photo album. An interesting unsolicited addition. It's clear a lot of work went into it."

"I find it's more common in the European milieu."

"Alors avant de commencer, êtes-vous à l'aise de converser en français dans un bureau au jour le jour?"

"Oh I don't speak French. I mean I understand it much more than I can speak it. I find that part a little harder."

"Well it says 'advanced proficiency' so perhaps it should read…"

"Intermediate?"

"Beginner?"

"Correct."

"Would you say you're more of a process-oriented or task-oriented person? You can only choose one."

"Task. No process! Process for sure. That's a hard one."

"Speaking of, one of the most difficult parts of the job is assessment and review. It says you have 'extensive experience in appraisal management'. Can you provide us with three examples where you achieved successful outcomes giving feedback to multiple stakeholders?"

"Pass."

"You want to pass?"

"Yes I'll pass on that one for sure."

"Turning to other languages, it says you 'executed a successful linguistic project in a cross-cultural context'."

"I learned Thai backpacking in Asia. It's an extremely complicated language, actually a set of languages."

"How long did you study?"

"Three weeks. But that was total immersion."

"I see."

"My real job is being in a band. So I read music also. That's a language in itself of course. So I'm a great team player and I know how to dominate very difficult personalities."

"Indeed. What is your biggest weakness?"

"That's tough. People say I am just too committed to my work. I work too many hours. I work too hard."

"Strengths?"

"Communications. Organization. Listening skills. Successful outcomes. Sorry was that a question?"

"Where do you see yourself in five years' time?"

"In the exact same position, absolutely."

"And this is the correct email that we should use? Thoughtleader_82@aol.com?"

"Yes. I'm still evaluating my options but this does sound like a great fit."

"Really. It says you're a '*committed buongustaio*' at the bottom of your resume."

"Yes I am."

"Can you tell me how to make a Roman carbonara?"

"Eggs. And...bacon?"

“Guanciale.”

“I didn’t know that.”

“Quelle surprise.”

The Impeachment of Macbeth
Edward Belfar

Treasonous dogs all,
They rise against me:
Kent, Taylor, the miner's daughter, Hill;
Morrison, Volker, and Vindman,
Who in dress uniform
Cloaks his disloyalty;
The she-devil Yovanovitch,
Who rages against me
And suffers not my portrait
To hang in its rightful place;
Even Sondland, erstwhile friend,
Whom now I hardly know,
Once eager to act at my direction,
Bears tales of quid pro quo.

I want nothing.
I want nothing.
I want no quid pro quo.
Just a favor from Zelensky,
In return for which,
If I am in the giving vein
When he calls upon me,
I may grant him audience
In that venerable Oval that I,
The Chosen One,
Blessed by Franklin Graham,
Have sanctified by my presence.

But the failing New York Times,
The Amazon Washington Post,
And Blitzer and Maddow
And Tapper and Tur
Malign and defame me,
Call me boorish and corrupt.
And who doth defend me?
Three stooges merely:
One an Ohio congressman,
Full of sound and fury,
Signifying nothing.
The second, a dolt from the west,

A pretend dairy farmer
Who, crying libel,
Sued an imaginary cow.
The third, the worst of them all,
A sniveling, bootlicker from Carolina
A serviceable villain,
Who sells his loyalty cheap
As a strumpet on a shithole street.
All three pay me counterfeit obeisance,
While minding but their own advancement.
They strut and fret their hour on Fox,
Goading the rabble to a frothing distemper,
But in the halls of the Capitol,
When some fake newsmonger,
With microphone in hand,
Dares them to defend my honour,
They scuttle to the nearest elevator
And then are heard no more.

From *Recipes for Inclusive Education,* Chapter 6, "Braises and Roasts"

Ingrid Tischer

Nature and her master THE LORD have blessed the Educator with ease in beginning any recipe for inclusion, 'Step One of How to Cook a Disabled Child: Catch a Disabled child.' Truly, the Infirm Child's enfeeblement makes him an ideal choice for the inexperienced Educator new to his twin masters Efficiency and Economy.

When you have your specimen, consider your various cooking options as well as how many Normal Children you have to feed. Is the Infirm Child plump and well-larded? If this be the case, wrap the lad's loin with the finest bacon and roast in a hot oven, a dish fit to serve at term's end to celebrate the holiday.

Far from protesting, many an Infirm Child's eyes shine with an Inner Light at mention of this most noble purpose their otherwise wasted bodies can serve. There are Disabled Children not as wholly selfish as their Disabled brethren who would demand survival, even education and employment, at the expense of their Normal brothers. But good it is to look upon the Infirm Child going cheerfully to the cook-pot to feed the strength of the Normal Child whose rude health is testament to his good character and his Creator's Pleasure in him.

Do not scorn the restauranteur's habit of presenting Monday's least-loved dishes as Saturday's "Specials." Only you will glimpse the curious truth of calling what was patently rejected a name denoting fond regard.

It is well to resist any temptation to avail yourself of the Infirm Child's mature counterparts that many a monger sets out near market's close. These Disabled Adults make poor eating as a rule. Often tough and stringy, what sustenance bitter and tastes of bile and other vile humors.

As the Infirm Child is carried securely within the Normal Children's innards, he will go far beyond where his withered limbs and ghastly countenance would have confined him, in that most detestable and costly of prison-houses, his own and tarnished flesh. Safely within his shining Brother, he will be seated in the classroom, play in the schoolyard, and finally, swing his feet carelessly as he sits inside the privy. All once beyond any hope of his reach but now gloriously attained by his inclusion in the school's menu. At mere pennies per serving.

Rest well, Educator, in the knowledge that you have served Efficiency and Economy well, your first duty as a servant of the public purse.

Phonography
Matt Gold

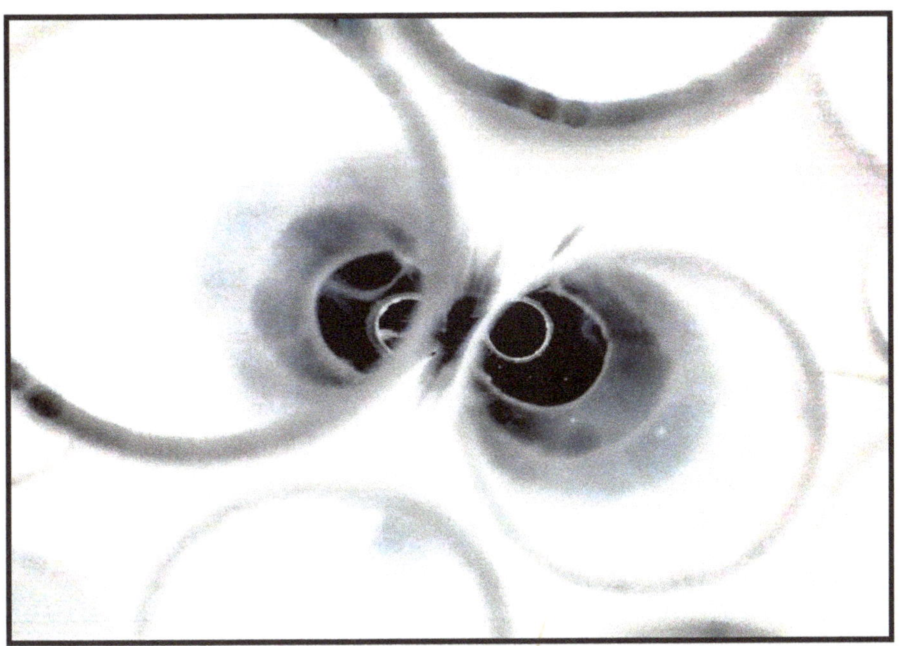

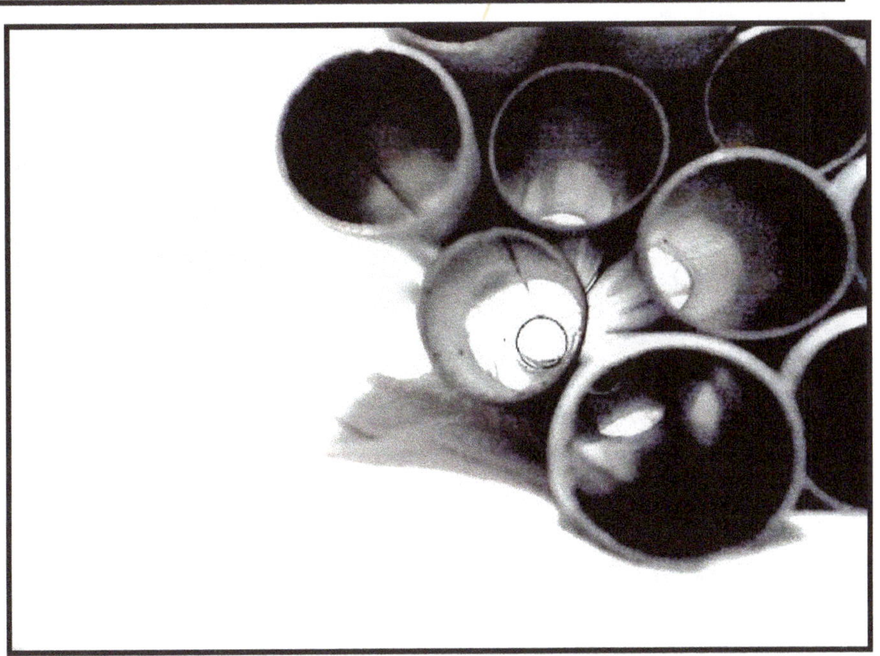

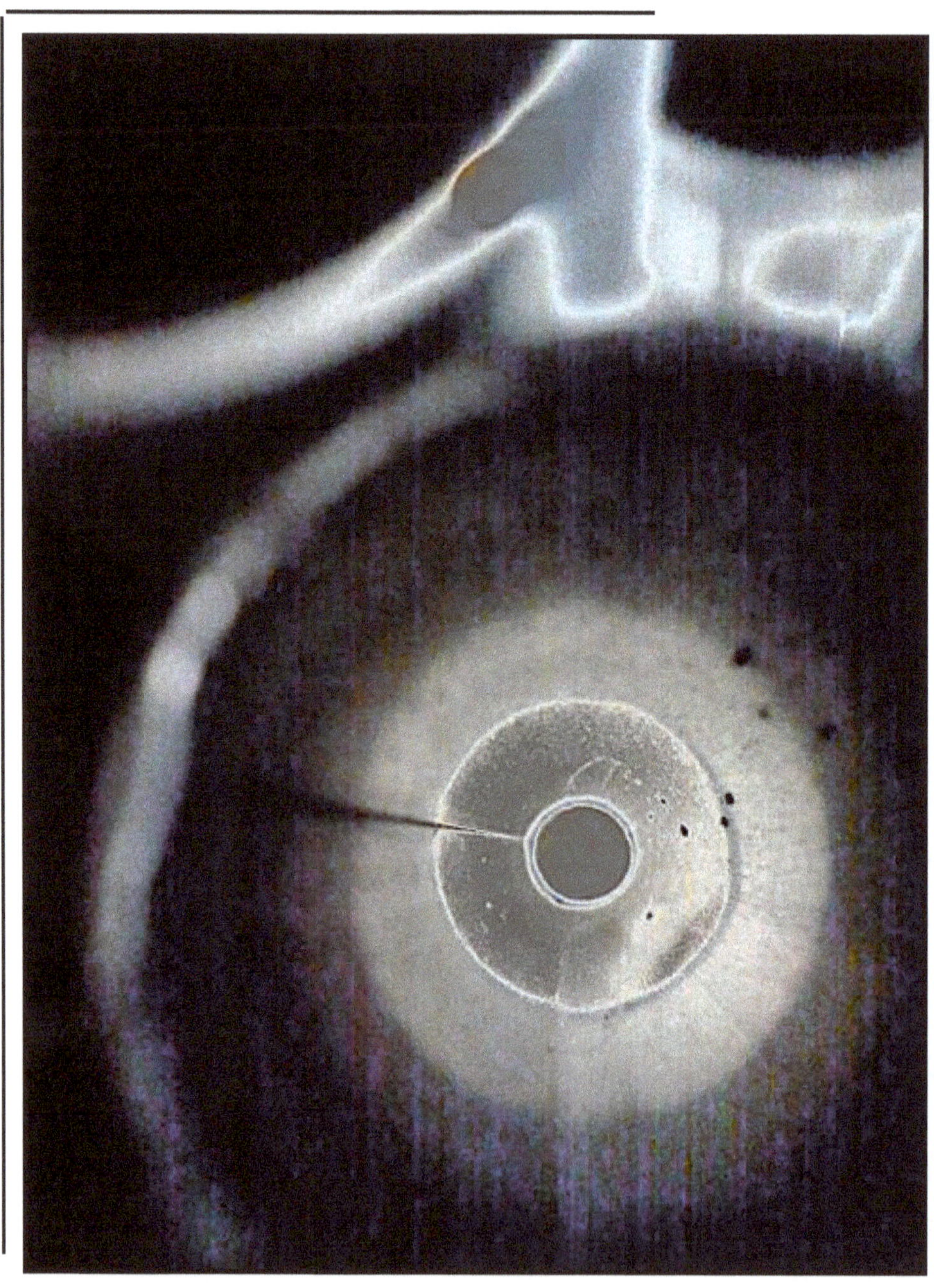

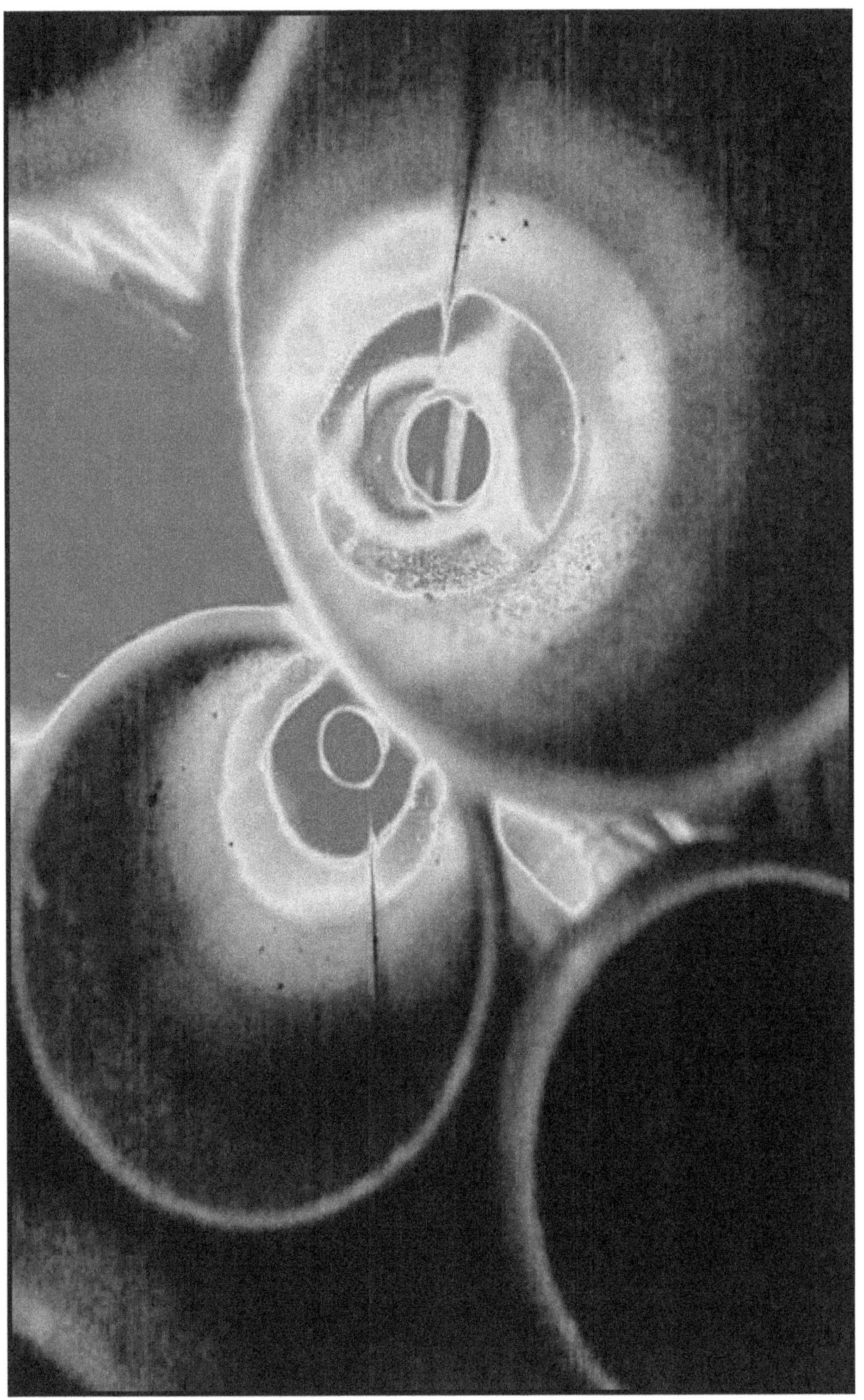

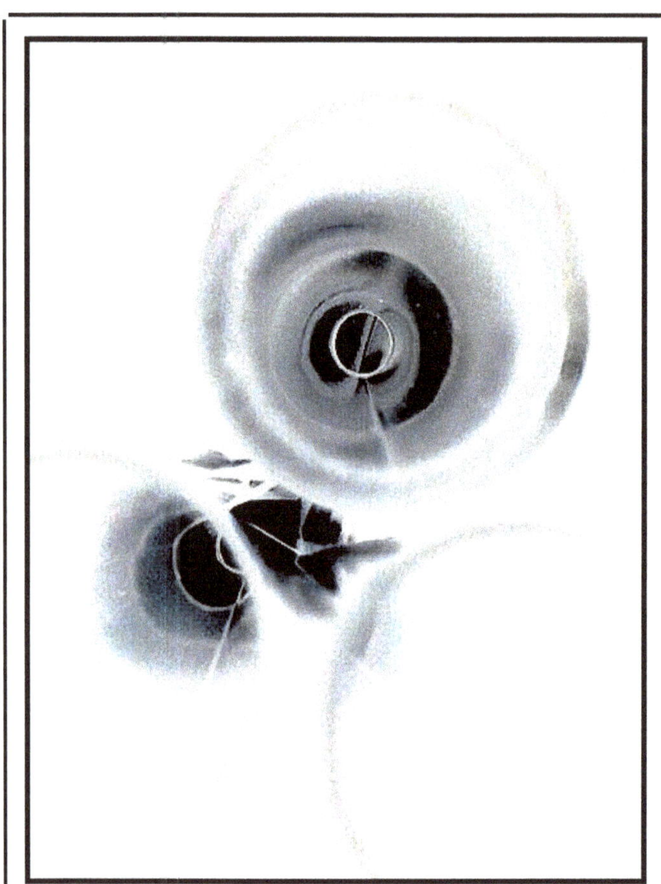

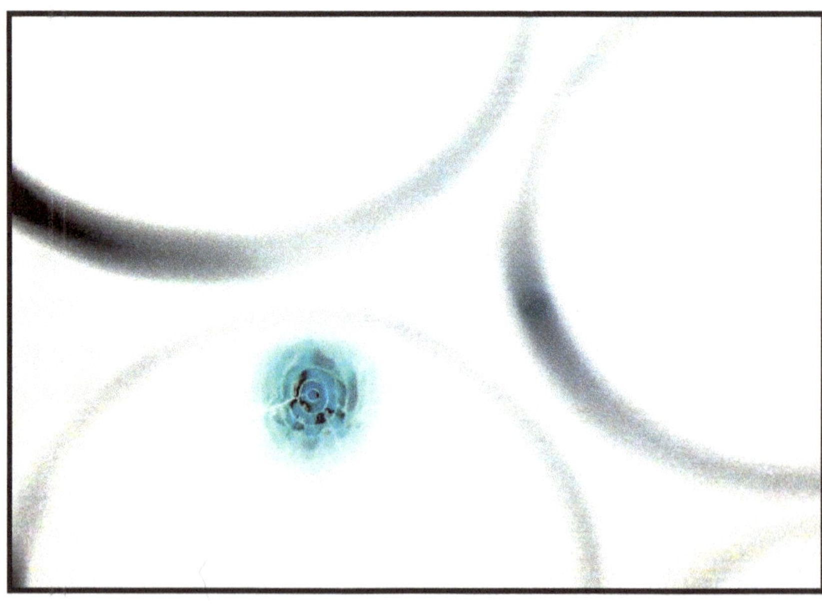

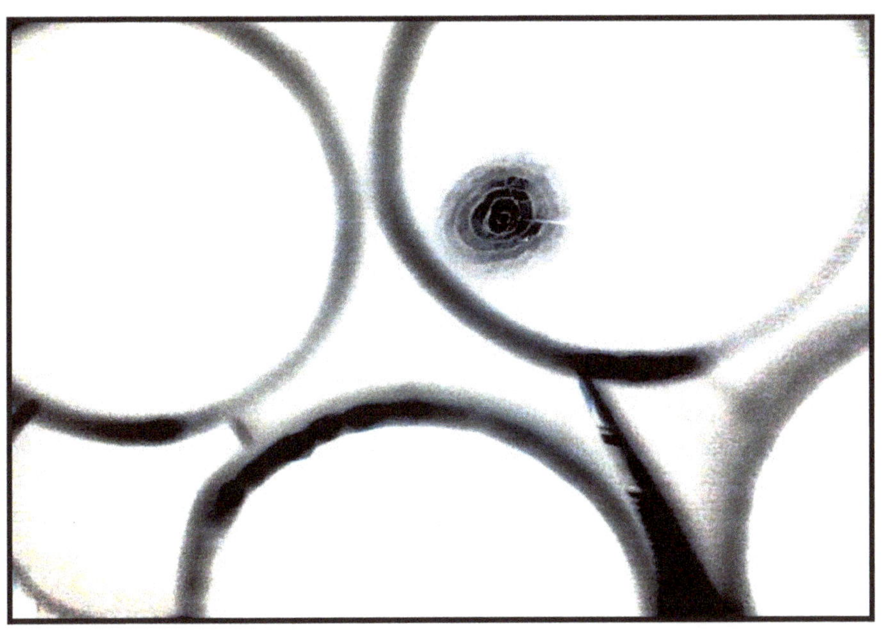

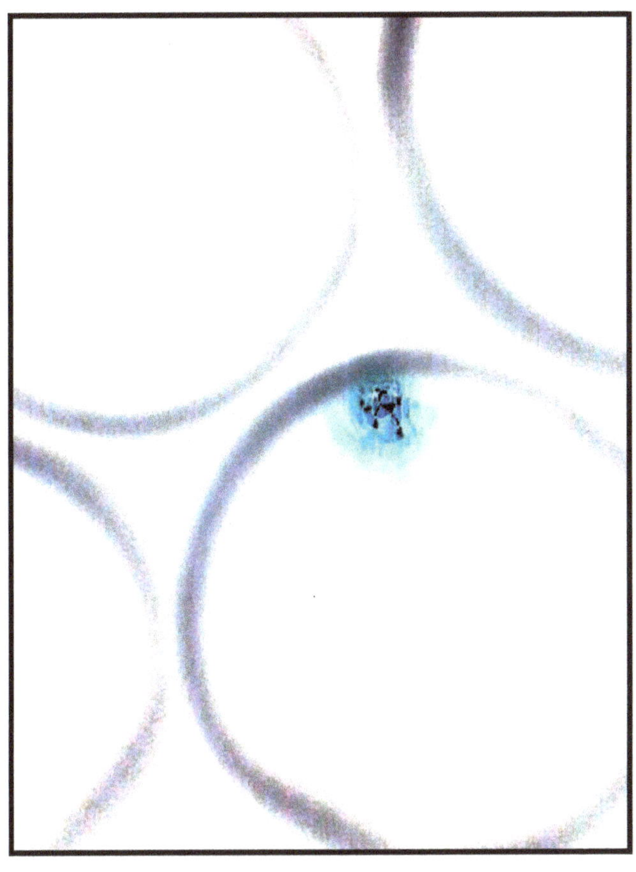

Sunrise Hike at Weldon Springs Conservation Area

Hannah Dains

Maybe god is in the fingers of sunlight
that reach through the branches
before the sun itself has risen,
something I can see with my eyes half closed
as I am falling asleep sitting against a tree
because I woke up at four in the morning
to watch the river light up gold
and the trees go from gray to green
as we sit and pretend that we can stay like this forever.
I think god is in the way my friend
fills silently with joy as I point out a bird
on a distant branch; when
we both realize it's a cardinal at the same time.
I think god is in the way my friend's phone
has not yet lit up to tell him his brother has died
and instead, he is laughing among the leaves,
bathed in sunlight, now,
the birds singing
the way he hasn't since.

Reading Adrienne Rich in Late December in Vermont, High on Cold and Flu Medications and Brokenhearted

Amanda Leahy

Room, crisis, trophies, bird-
wings,

walls, everything
severed: Tell me,

who would live
in this place

without some kind of
language

or, at least, a dream
in the shape of one?

Fantasy

Nam Nguyen

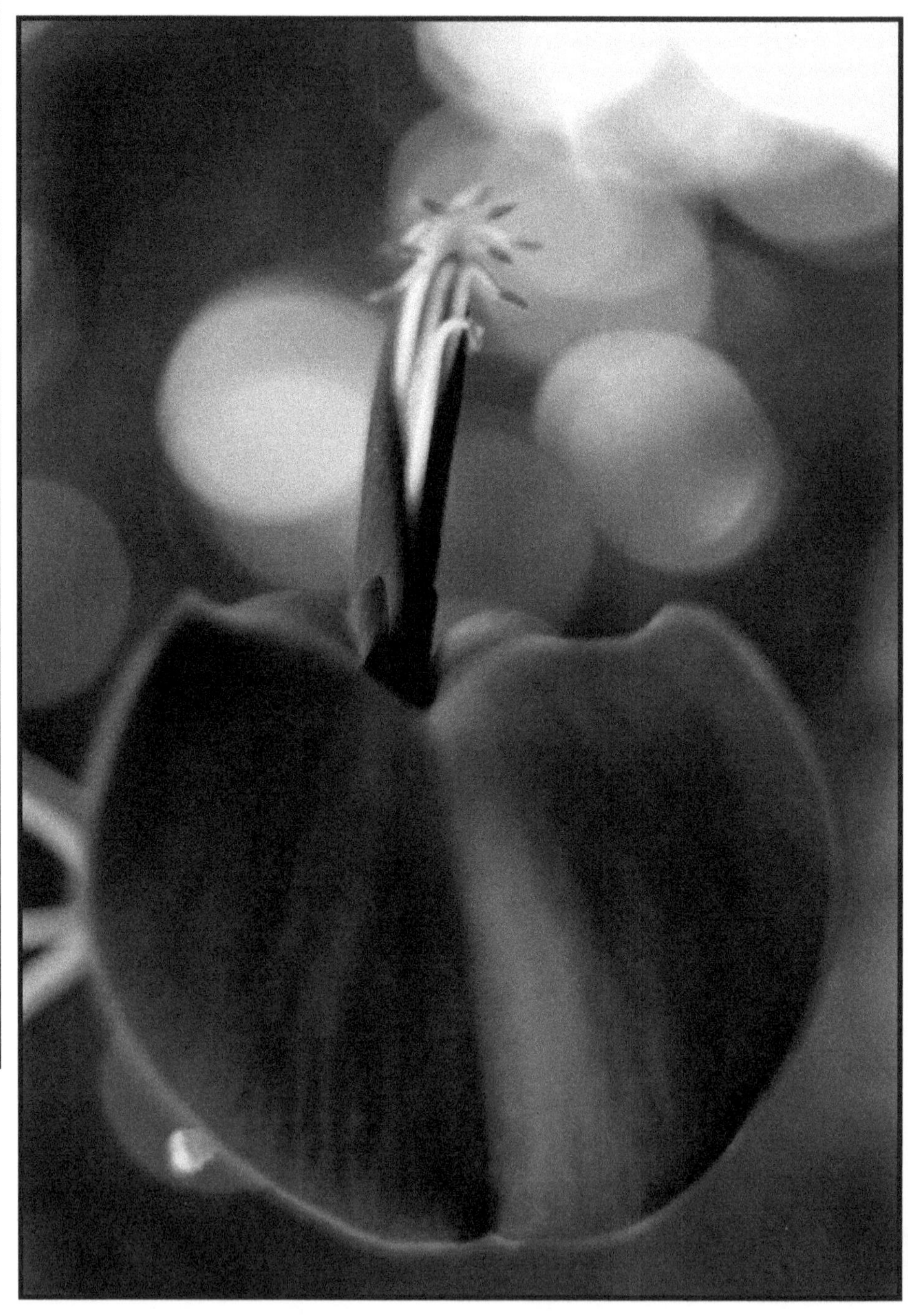

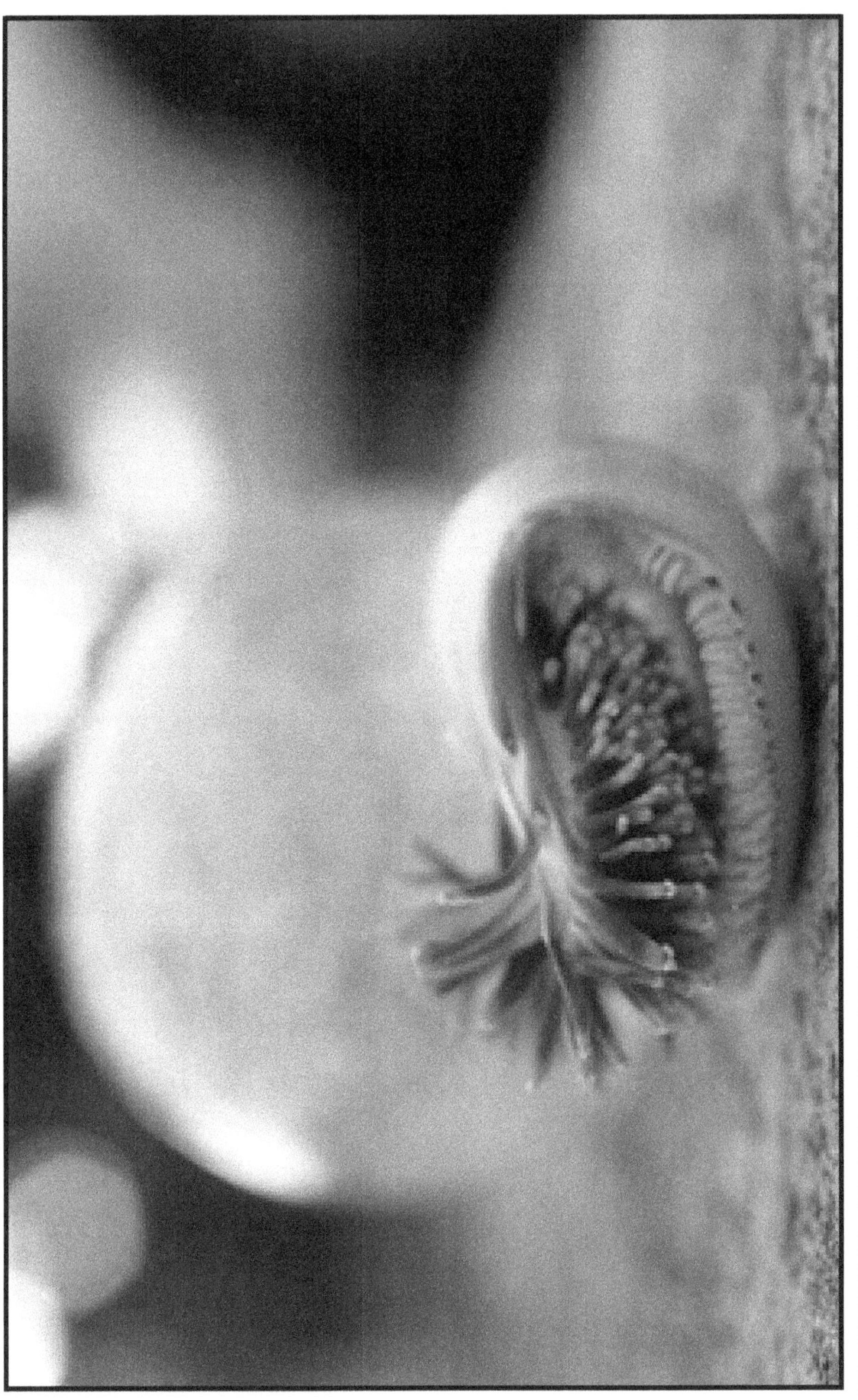

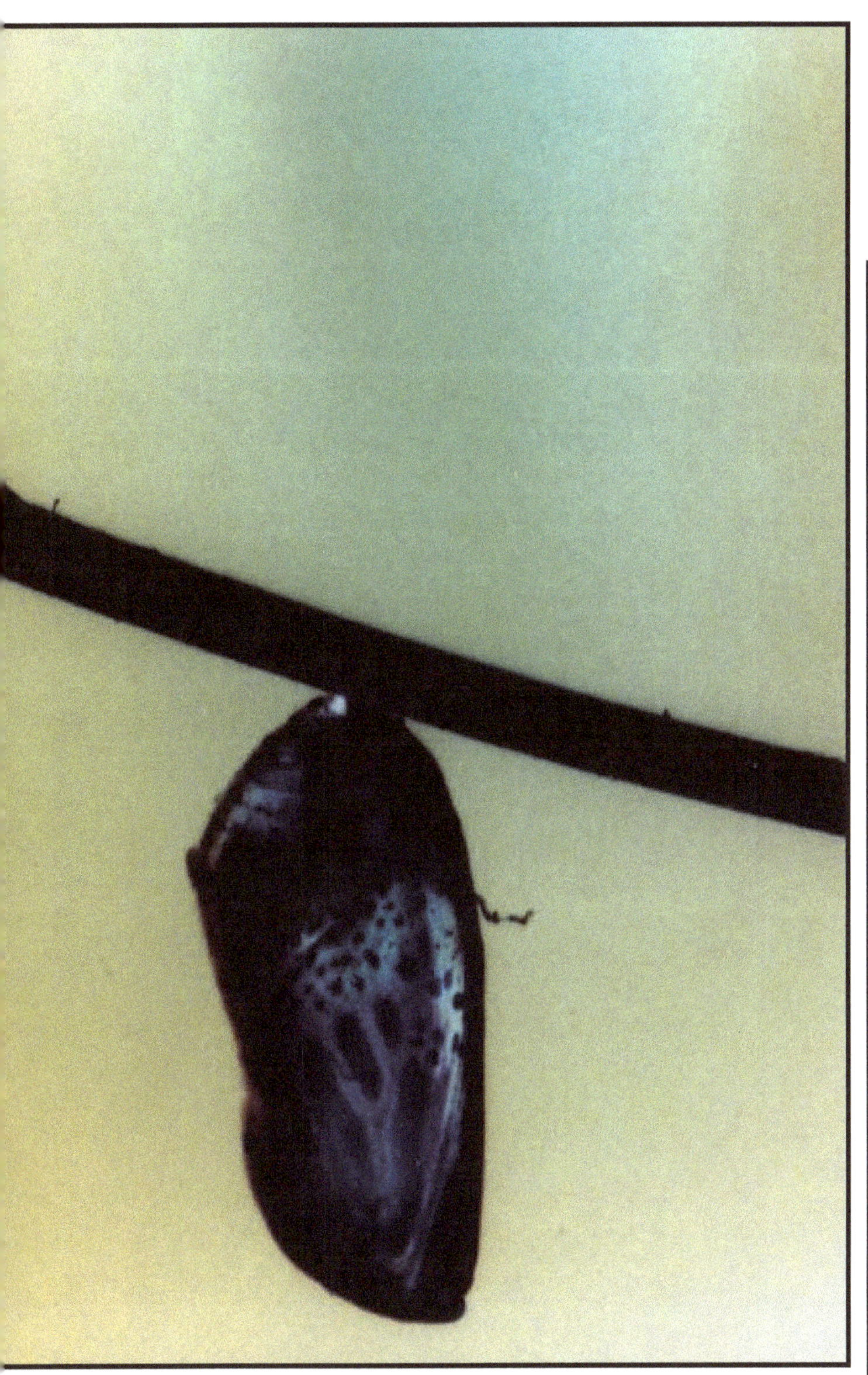

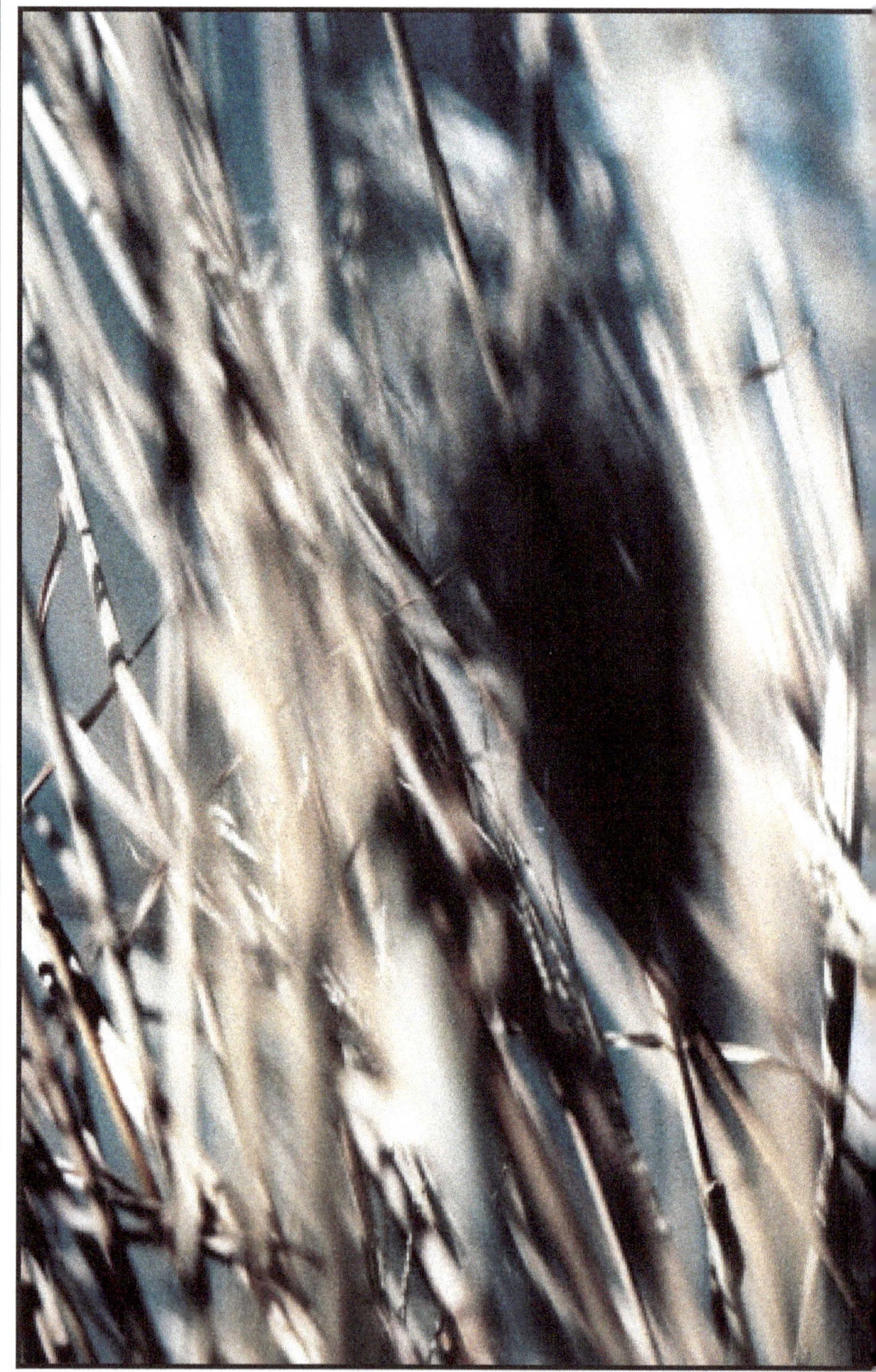

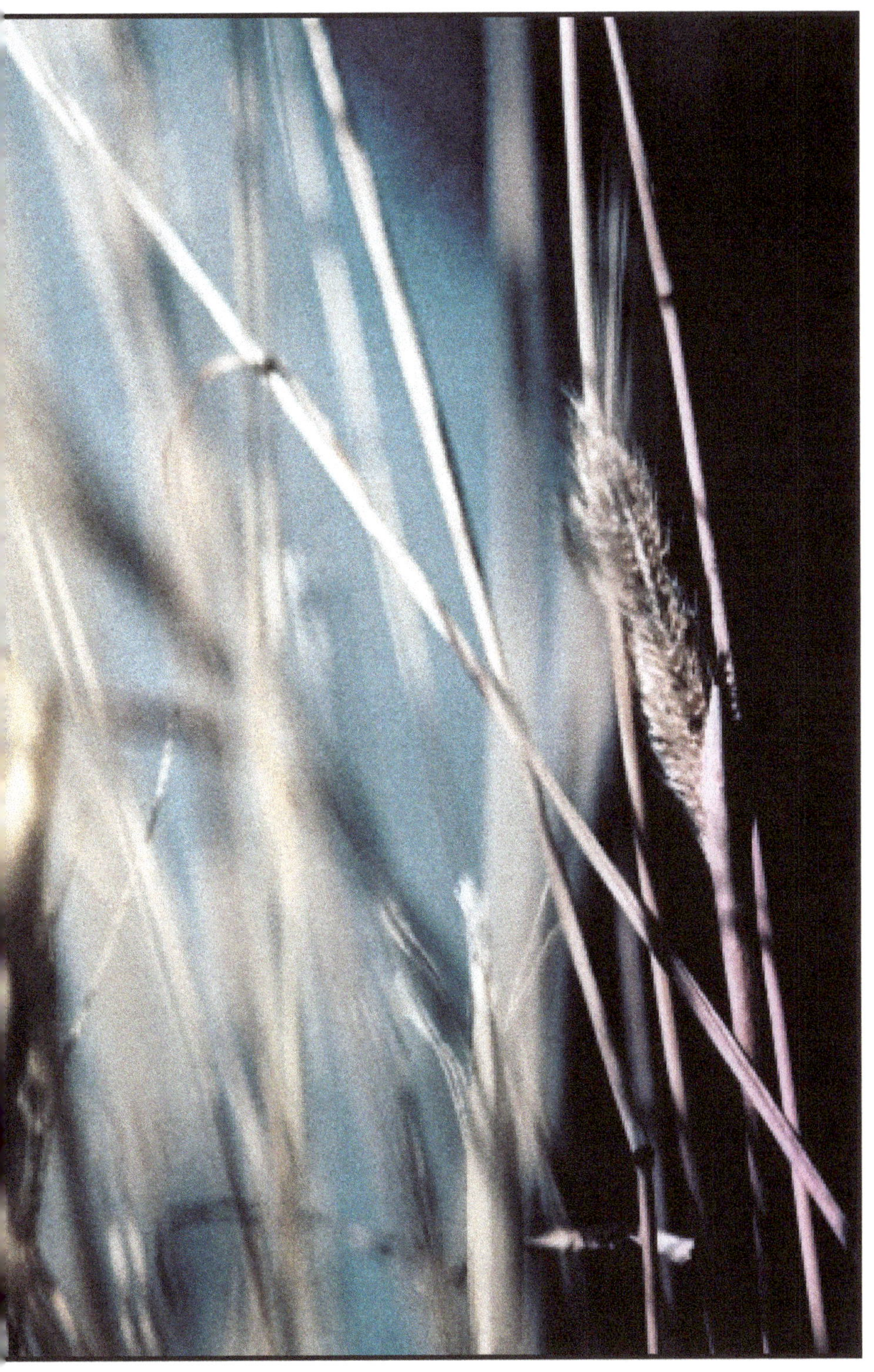

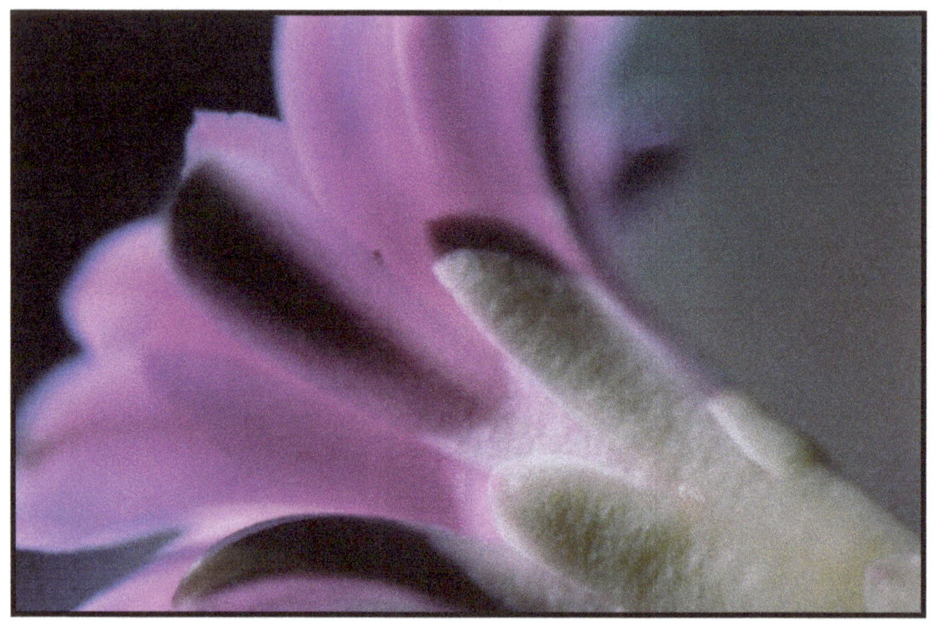

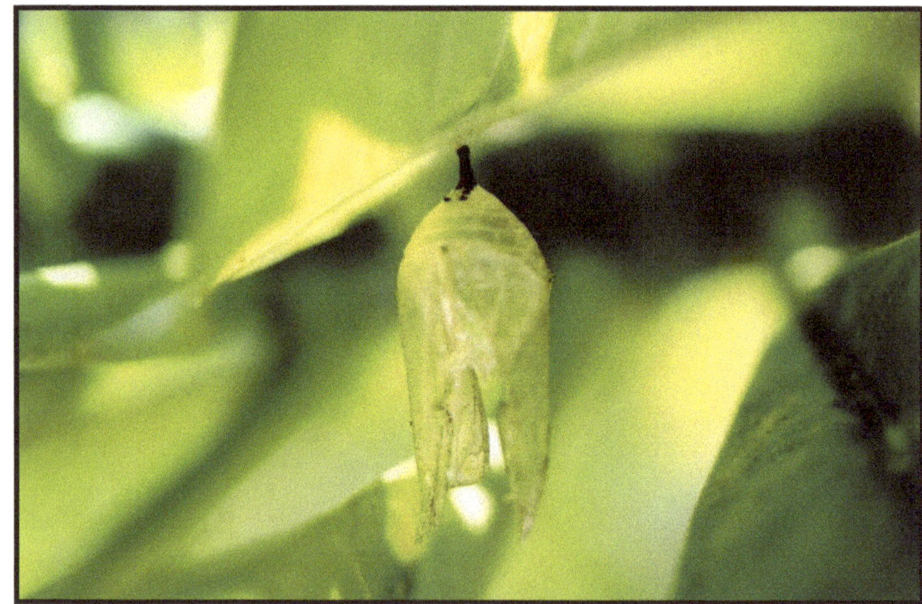

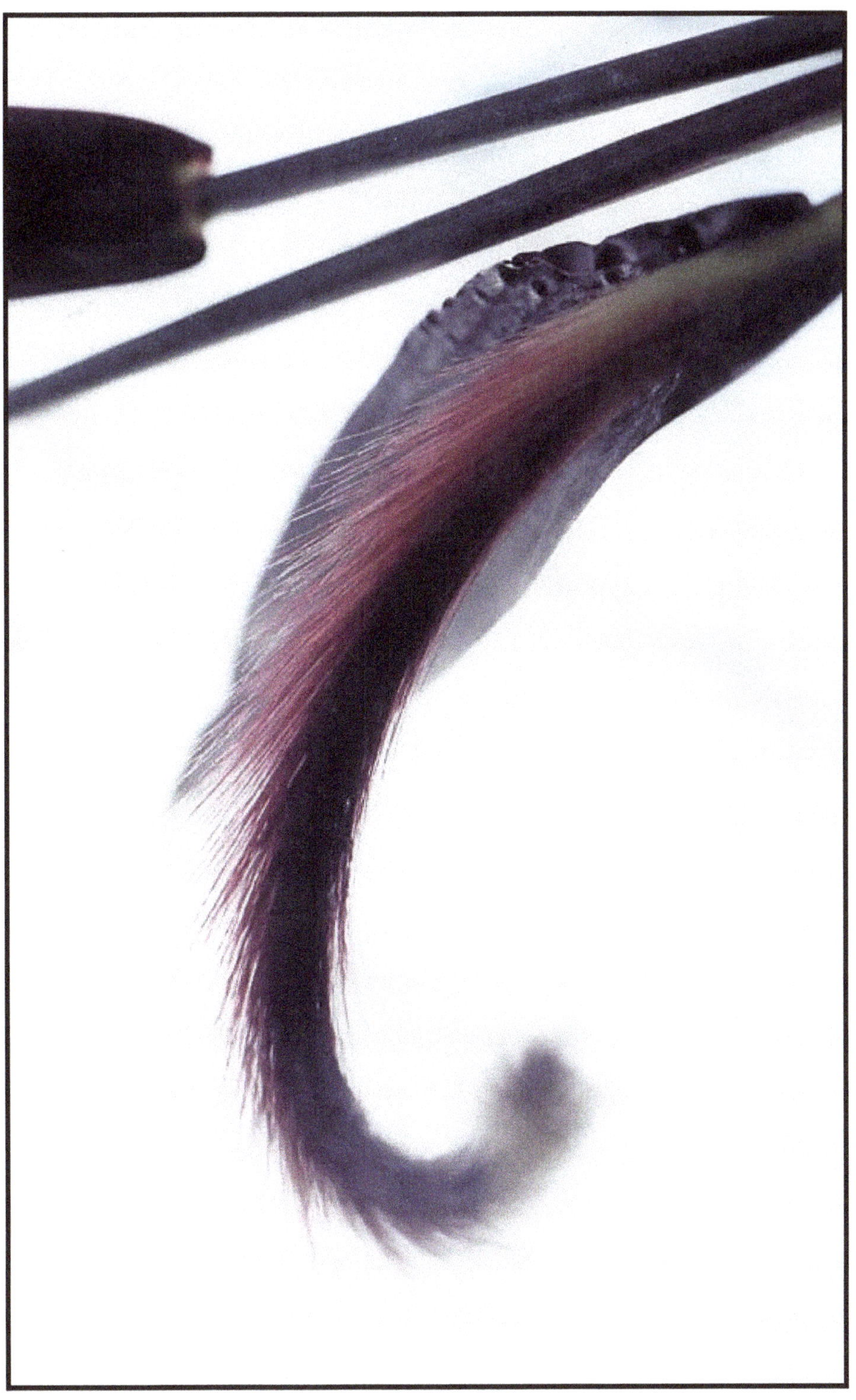

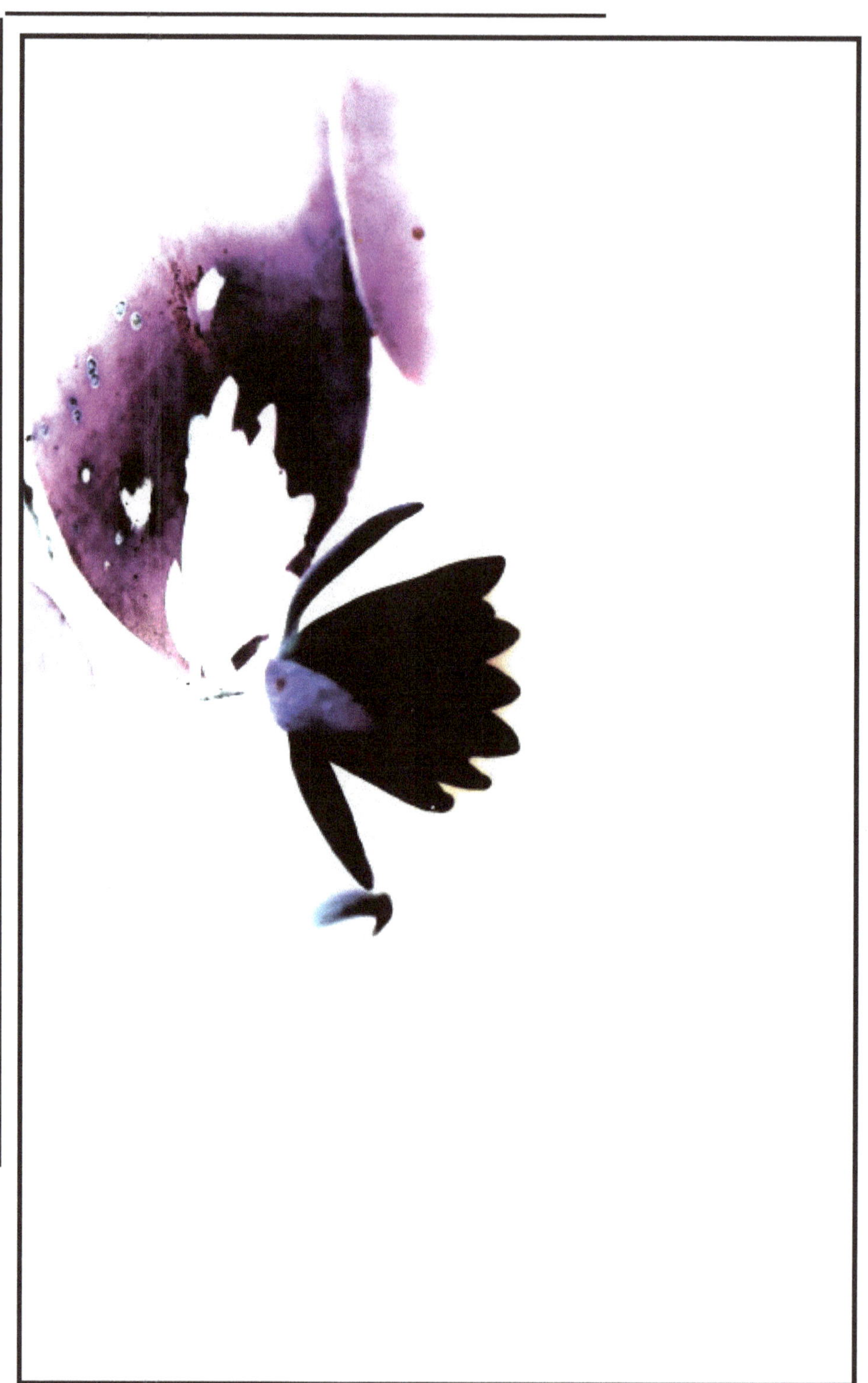

Dumpster Fire

Clark Boyd

Eddie Bigelow had seen dumpster fires before, but only virtual ones. To him, they were nothing but funny pictures or GIFs, convenient ways to poke fun at the latest scandals in Washington or Hollywood. They appeared on social media as if by magic with snarky captions like "Actual Footage," or "Burn Baby Burn!"

But now Eddie was staring at a real dumpster fire across the street from his apartment.

He tossed his still-lit cigarette on the ground, not bothering to grind it out. He then reached for his phone. He had to get a video of this. The fire was small, but the flames bright and intense. Eddie thought maybe there were chemicals in the dumpster; the flames licking their way up the rusted sides were so colorful. He couldn't look away.

Eddie knew, instinctively, that this would look good online. Especially in HD.

From the other side of the street, he began filming. In his excitement, he tried to hold the phone steady. He was already plotting the target of his virtual vitriol. He hated the Mets. They always qualified as a dumpster fire. Republicans, democrats, libertarians—all complete disasters these days. Eddie was sure the girl who lived next door to him was cooking meth in her apartment. That was a real-life dumpster fire. But Jill followed him online, and he wasn't sure outing her was worth it. Even though it would be incredibly satisfying.

As Eddie pondered, the fire grew in intensity. It filled the phone's entire screen now. Tilting the device upward, Eddie's eye followed the smoke, which was now leeching into the blue sky. Black and blue? Black on blue? It had potential, he thought.

At that moment, Jill and her boyfriend, "Skeevy Stevie," entered Eddie's frame. He couldn't believe his luck. It was a cool autumn day, and Jill's hands were stuffed deep into the pockets of her coat. Her eyes were red. Eddie wondered if it was tears, the drugs, or both. Next to her, Stevie carried a phone. He was pointing manically at the screen and yelling at Jill. As the couple approached the burning dumpster, Eddie could faintly hear a profane duet of "fuck you's."

As content went, this was promising. Eddie hoped that Jill and Stevie would suddenly stop and stare at the fire with their (possibly) drug-addled eyes. He could then zoom in and capture the exact moment the fog cleared and they realized what they were seeing. Maybe one of them would scream. Eddie envisioned all the replies from his Twitter followers, who would love making fun of the vapid, terrified looks on the faces of these two tweakers.

But Jill and Stevie were so involved in their argument they didn't even notice the dumpster fire. They walked right past it without a glance and moved on. As they did so, they stepped around Mrs. Crispin, who was headed in the opposite direction pushing her newborn in a stroller. She was deep in conversation on her phone. On his screen, Eddie noticed her furrowed brow and the worry lines around her eyes. He figured that, as a caring mother, Mrs. Crispin would definitely notice the fire and move to the other side of the street with her baby. But instead, she put her head down and calmly pushed the stroller through the smoke. She never stopped talking.

Eddie kept filming.

Five more people from the neighborhood walked by without acknowledging the dumpster fire. All of them were pecking away on phones or tablets. Eddie watched as the flames crept still higher. They were now dangerously close to the second-floor windows of a nearby apartment building. The only thing Eddie could hear around him was the soft crackle of the fire, punctuated from time to time by the loud bang of an aerosol can exploding in the dumpster. On his screen, not a single head turned at the noise.

Eddie stopped filming.

He checked the memory on his phone and realized he might have to erase what he'd recorded so far, but that didn't bother him. Eddie was frustrated. People weren't responding the way he expected them to, the way he *wanted* them to. There was nothing remotely viral about his entire neighborhood completely ignoring this potentially dangerous event. There were no shocked faces, no screams of "Holy shit!" No one had made a funny comment like, "So...that's a *real* dumpster fire." No one else was even filming it.

Then Eddie saw Mr. Rayburn walking up the street. He quickly deleted the old file from his phone and started filming again.

Mr. Rayburn entered from the left, then stopped and leaned on his cane. He looked at the fire with an appropriate combination of shock and horror. Finally, thought Eddie. After an ominous pop, the old man took two steps back, raising his hand to shield his face.

Eddie could sense this might be the moment he'd been waiting for. Old man Rayburn in the left third of the shot, the fire center-right with the flames stretching up to the top of the phone and then out of the frame. All he needed now was for this crotchety old bastard to start screaming in fear. Or crying, Eddie thought. That would be even better.

Instead, Mr. Rayburn looked away from the dumpster fire and stared directly at Eddie's phone. Then back at the fire. And then back at the phone again.

"You that Bigelow kid?"

"Yeah."

"Is that one of those cameras that's also a phone?"

"Yes, sir."

"I don't have one of those."

"Too bad. It's really handy in situations like this," Eddie said.

"I'll bet. Hey, could you do me a favor?"

"Sure."

"Could you stop filming and use that damn thing to get the fire department over here to put this fucker out?"

Eddie hit pause on the video, and then stared blankly at his screen.

d"It's easy," said Mr. Rayburn. "Just dial 9-1-1."

Dream

Photography by Nikita Petrov
Poetry by Raymond Byrnes

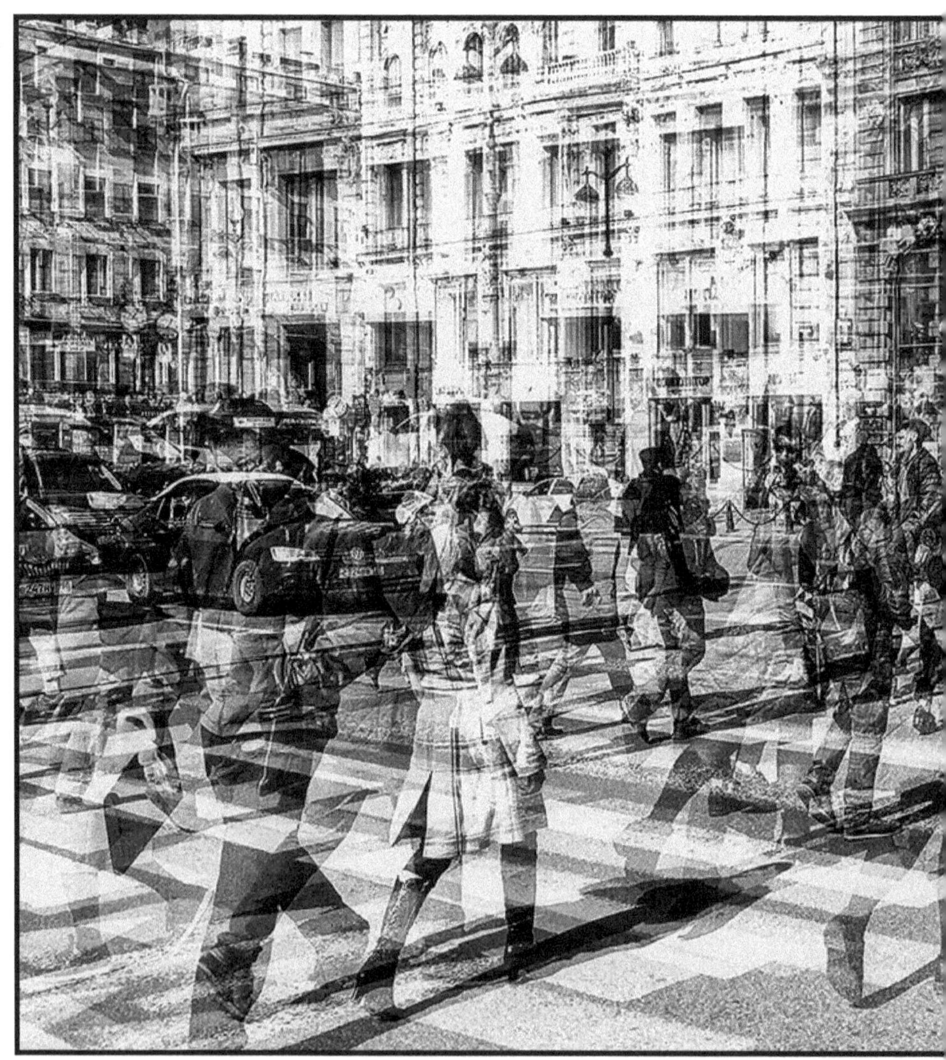

He relishes every random nap, content in his
awareness that now no one in the universe
will be concerned how he spends his next
half hour or if his phone remains in sleep mode.

Lately, he reads gritty memoirs from the South
murders solved by Harry Bosch, sports biographies
histories of how The Great War shaped his world
poems that make him tap his lips and read again.

Sometimes when dozing, he dreams he's running
late; can't find the hallway for Conference Room
907B; didn't grab his laptop; has nothing ready
to present if asked; phone's down to 1%.

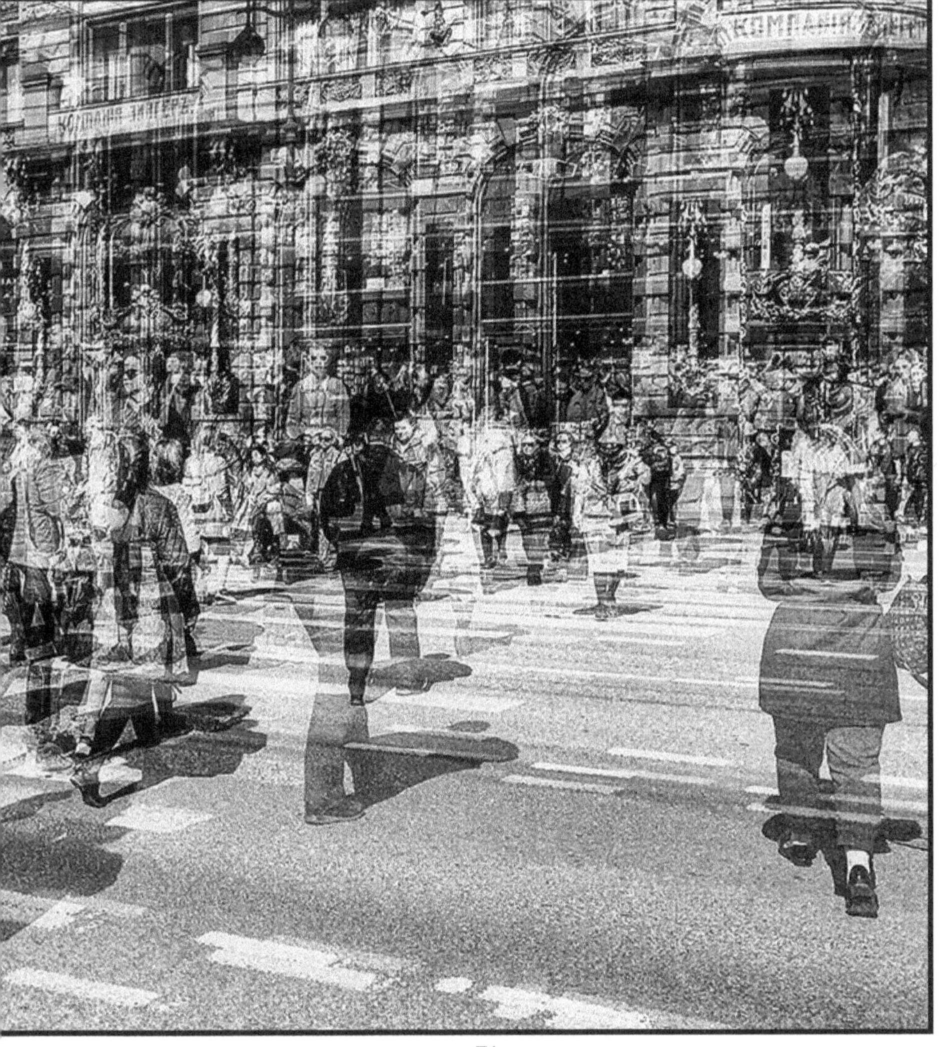

In Order Of Appearance:

Rashad Wright is the Poet Laureate of Jersey City, New Jersey. He is a graduate of New Jersey City University, receiving his BA in English: Creative Writing. On campus he was most known for his work with Peers Educating Peers (PEP) as a certified peer educator. Outside of NJCU, Rashad's poetry has been heard from both local and national stages via slam poetry. He is the only person to be titled the "Grandslam Champion of Jersey City Slam" twice. He has also competed in the 2015 National Poetry Slam in Oakland, California then again in the 2017 National Poetry Slam in Denver, Colorado. Since 2016 he has also coached Jersey City Slam. Also at the 2017 Individual World Poetry Slam in Spokane, Washington Rashad won 25th in the country. He also coached the 2019 6th Borough He has been awarded: First Place for the Walter Glospie American Academy of Poets Prize. Outside of poetry Rashad's work expands into memoir, fiction, short story, performance art, and music. His work has been published in several online magazines and journals. He is currently working on a book length manuscript titled Working Definition: Dictionary & Thesaurus and a poetry album titled Romeo's Whiskey.

Henry Stanton's fiction, poetry and paintings have been widely published internationally and have recently appeared in Alien Buddha Press, Chicago Record, Down In The Dirt Magazine, High Shelf Press, Holy & Intoxicated Press, Kestrel, North of Oxford, Outlaw Poetry, The Paragon Press, PCC Inscape, Ramingo!, Rusty Truck, Salt & Syntax, Under The Bleachers, The William and Mary Review, The Write Launch and Yellow Mama. His book of Short Stories, "River of Sleep and Dreams" is due to be published by Alien Buddha Press in 2020. His book of poems "The Man Who Turned Stuff Off" was published by Holy & Intoxicated Press in June 2019 and a second book of poetry, "Pain Rubble" is due to be published by Holy & Intoxicated Press in early 2020. His poetry was selected for the A3 Review Poetry Prize and was shortlisted for the Eyewear 9th Fortnight Prize for Poetry. His fiction received an Honorable Mention acceptance for the Salt & Syntax Fiction Contest and was selected as a finalist for the Pen 2 Paper Annual Writing Contest. A selection of Henry Stanton's paintings will be on show at Atwater's Catonsville on March 25, 2020 (other shows to be announced) and can be viewed at the following website www.brightportfal.com. A selection of Henry Stanton's published fiction and poetry can be located for reading in the library at www.brightportfal.com. Henry Stanton is Publisher of Uncollected Press and the Founding & Managing Editor of The Raw Art Review – www.therawartreview.com

Kristin Withers is a poet currently residing in the Pacific Northwest. She has occupied a spectrum of collared, color collared, & non-collared vocational posts. Disciplined in analytic philosophy her interests focus on epistemology & the metaphysics of consciousness. Her poetry appears (or will) at Chiron Review, High Shelf Press, & The Inquisitive Eater, amongst others. She is currently working a gallery in liminal nocturnes & a collection of autoscopic language poetry.

Cree Cullars is an emerging Writer, Artist, & Energy Healer.

Emily Capers currently lives in Chicago, IL. She is a second-year student at Columbia College Chicago where she's earning her MFA in Fiction Writing. Her work typically explores the topic of identity while experimenting with form. Emily has two pieces of short fiction published in Baldwin Wallace University's literary journal The Mill.

Erin Bennett holds a BA in Creative Writing from Colby-Sawyer College. She will begin courses for a Masters of Liberal Studies, focused in creative writing, this winter, 2019. Erin currently lives in the village of Taftsville, Vermont.

Zoltan Kegyes is a hungarian writer and visual artist, currently living and studying in Maastricht. He works with collage techniques, geometrical forms, minimalistic, and colorful designs. As a writer he is exploring the free flowing poetic speech structures of the villagers he grew up with. He likes the color red.

Stephen Herman: MFA in Creative Writing/Poetry, U. Mass., Amherst. Taught Creative Writing/Poetry for 12 years at City College of San Francisco. Published Night Visions in 2012, awarded Gold Seal of Literary Excellence. First Prize in Poetry, 2013, SF Writers' Conference. SF Human Rights Commissioner for 2 years.

Heather Quinn is a poet living in San Francisco who loves the act of layering memory, imagination, images, the political & spiritual into her work. She often thinks of writing as collage-making. Recent and upcoming publishing credits are 42 Miles Press, Burning House Press, Ghost City Review, Headline Poetry & Press, Kissing Dynamite, Prometheus Dreaming & Raw Art Review. You can find her on Twitter at @hquinnpoet www.heatherquinnpoet.com

Maddie is a painter and performer whose work has appeared all over New York City. She primarily works in the surprisingly similar mediums of acrylic paint and stand up comedy. However, she is also an improv and sketch comedian, illustrator and printmaker. Maddie graduated Sarah Lawrence College with a concentration in Art History and Theater and now works as a freelance illustrator and graphic designer. She was an honored alumni from Arquetopia Foundation's Artist-in-Residency program in 2017 in Puebla, Mexico and became a featured artist at Azule Artist in Residence program in North Carolina. She continues her practice in Brooklyn, NY and editions of her prints and one-of-a-kind clay pins can be found on her website: www.maddiefischer.com

Rob Martinez is a video director and writer living in New York. His fiction work has appeared in Lovers & Other Strangers, Breadcrumbs Magazine and Green Zebra magazine. His professional video work is almost always epicurean, and his personal video work is almost always imperfect.

Eros Livieratos studied philosophy and creative writing at William Paterson University. Eros' writing tackles topics of race, sexuality, capitalism, aesthetics, and technology. Eros plays in noise bands in New Jersey and can often be found yelling about aesthetics & automation in your local basement.

Ellis Scott's first short story "Levies" was published by Into The Void magazine in October 2019. He is nominated for the 2020 Pushcart Prize. He is queer and disabled.

Edward Belfar is the author of Wanderers, a collection of short stories published by Stephen F. Austin State University Press in 2012. His work has also appeared in a number of magazines, including Shenandoah, The Baltimore Review, Potpourri, Open Spaces, Confrontation, Natural Bridge, and Tampa Review.

Based in the Bay Area, Ingrid Tischer writes fiction, and disability culture and policy commentary. Her writing is a mix of the serious, the sardonic, and the sincere that uses personal essay, opinion, spoof, and parody forms to convey the emotional landscape of lifelong disability and the waxy bummer build-up that comes from ableism. She is an unpublished writer beyond her own blog, Tales From the Crip. She presents much of her fiction as "crip lit," which she defines as having at least one main character who is both disabled and aware of their disability's political dimension. She was a longtime member of San Francisco's Writing Circles for Women (1993-2001), attended Flight of the Mind fiction writing workshops in 1997, 1998, and 2000 taught by the novelists Charlotte Watson Sherman, Lynne Sharon Schwartz, and Gish Jen, respectively. In 2002-2003, she completed a fiction mentoring year with the novelist Lewis Buzbee through San Antonio's Gemini Ink. She worked privately with him from 2003-2007 and completed two drafts of a coming-of-middle-age novel currently titled "There's No Cure for Gretchen Lowe."

Matt Gold is based in Brooklyn, NY, where he divides his time between music and photography. As evidence of the democratizing nature of his approach to photography, Gold has no formal training in the visual arts. His first image, a picture of his cat on a Sony Ericsson Z310A flip phone, was taken in 2008, and he has continued to explore the aesthetic possibilities of that instrument, resisting the updated phones and apps available and revealing a contemporary nostalgia that encompasses the prolific imagery of our visual culture. Gold's work has been featured in numerous publications and journals

Hannah Dains is a senior at Washington University in St. Louis studying sociology, drama, and writing. When she isn't climbing trees and writing poems about it, she's producing experimental theater at her university as part of Thyrsus. Once she graduates in 2020, who knows.

Amanda Leahy is a native of Lowell, Massachusetts. She is currently an MFA candidate at Vermont College of Fine Arts and lives in Montpelier, Vermont. Her work has appeared in Thin Air, Crack the Spine, Pithead Chapel, and elsewhere.

Nam is a multimedia artist who explores the unexplored in his work.

Clark Boyd is a former journalist who spent two decades reporting, writing, editing, and producing international news for US public radio. He now lives in the Netherlands with his family. No, not in a windmill. clarkboyd on Instagram, @clark_boyd on Twitter.

Nikita Petrov was born in 1986 in Barnaul (Siberia, Russia). In 2010 graduated from The Altai State Technical University The Architecture and Design Institute. Since 2012 has been living and working in St.Petersburg (Russia).

Recent work by Raymond Byrnes has been read on The Writer's Almanac, featured as Editors' Choice in five journals, and published in Third Wednesday, Shot Glass Journal, Better Than Starbucks, Misfits, Typishly, and numerous other places. He lives in Virginia.

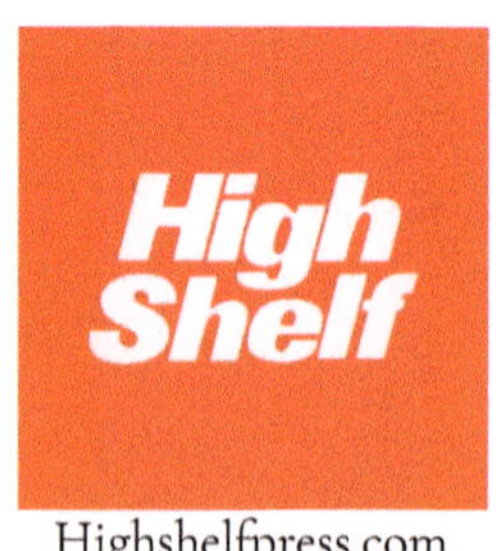

Highshelfpress.com